A Century Old

Mrs. Bailey,
Always cherish your past,
live in the present, and
hope for the future!
Thanks for your interest.

Rene Reed Gilliam '13

A Century Old

A journalist relives one hundred years through the memories of her grandmother

---

RENEE REED GILLIAM

LITTLE HOOT PUBLISHING

LITTLE HOOT PUBLISHING, LLC
MOORESVILLE, NORTH CAROLINA

Published by Little Hoot Publishing, LLC
littlehootpublishing@yahoo.com

Edited by Kyle Reynolds
Cover design by Little Hoot Publishing, LLC

ISBN 978-0-9884550-0-9

Printed in the United States of America

To Memaw
Her memory helped write this book.
May everyone who reads it be encouraged
and find happiness in everything
as she has.

Mildred at Martha Washington College in 1930

Mildred at Martha Washington Inn in 2008

Acknowledgments

To the Garrett children:
Carter Jr., Jimmy, Gene, Patty, and my mother Linda. She and my father Parvon deserve a big thanks for teaching me to love and cherish family.

To the memory of my grandfather, Carter Frank Garrett, my grandmother's one and only love. I now truly know what love is and I share that with my wonderful husband Jason to whom I thank for all his support during my writing venture.

To all of Mildred's grandchildren:
Carol Ann, Frank, Allen, Vickie, Angela, Mary, Janette, and in memory of Greg and Stephen.

To all the great-grandchildren:
Emily, Frankie, Marie, Brandon, Tommy, Stephanie, Spencer, Jennifer, Christopher, Adam, Kendall, Colin, Colson, and great-great-grandchildren Aiyana, Catherine, and Lillian.

To the Oma Hall family:
Six children, twelve grandchildren, eighteen great-grandchildren, and one great-great-grandchild, and in memory of Oma. My grandmother called them all her own.

I also want to dedicate my first book to my former teacher and friend, Barbara Hollis. I never break a promise. Thank you for always encouraging me to write.

Contents

Introduction

I grew up in the hills of Northeast Tennessee, raised as an only child in the 1980's and 90's. In decades when kids were listening to hip hop and rock and watching MTV, I was listening to Elvis and the oldies and watching *Little House on the Prairie* and *The Waltons.*

My father was fifty-six years old when I was born and my mother thirty-four. However, the twenty-two years difference in their ages did not make my life different from any other kid my age. My father was married before he married my mother. His first wife died of cancer. He fell in love with my mother a couple years later, and I guess you could say it was love at first sight. My mother says he was very persistent. I later saw that same kind of relationship in my own marriage. I was very close to my mother and father and had special and different relationships with each of them.

Since my parents were a little older than most, I learned to appreciate the older ways of living. I had a wonderful and vivid imagination. I could play with a cardboard box and have just as much fun as I could have with a new toy made from the plastic era. A tomboy, I loved to play outside and did not mind getting dirty, but when I was inside everything had its place and always stayed there.

I had only one living grandparent, and when I was two years old, she moved closer to us. From then until the present she lived only two miles away from my parents. It made the visits for me very frequent, and my relationship with my maternal grandmother, who I call "Memaw," was like a relationship with another parent. I was always packing my bags to spend the night with her or calling her on the phone asking, "Guess what Memaw?"

She was a playmate and confidant. I would tell her anything

and she would always understand. She played with me just like another child would. We would draw and paint, play games, house, doctor, and school. She would watch movies with me and we would eat pizza and banana splits.

Other than my parents, she was the only family I had living close to me. We took her on family vacations with us, and she attended the same church we did. She was seventy-two years old when I was born. I was the youngest grandchild and the only one who lived close to her. As years went by, my feelings for my grandmother changed from the affection felt for a playmate to the admiration of a woman of great strength and determination. No matter how well or unwell she felt, she always pushed herself to go to ball games, Girl Scout programs, and band concerts. As she got older she started pushing herself more often, and at the age of ninety-eight she traveled with my uncle and two aunts to see my husband and me in Meridian, Mississippi, after a long trip they took to Branson, Missouri.

This book holds memories she has passed on to me of her one hundred years of life. She was born in 1911 and this is the year 2011. What better way to take a trip into history than to hear about it through the memories of one who lived it? I am now a journalist, and was partially inspired by my grandmother and her habit of keeping a diary. She passed that habit on to my mother and now on to me. I have kept one since I was in the first grade and I sold enough wrapping paper in a school fundraiser that I got to choose a prize, and I chose a diary.

As a journalist, I live by knowing that history repeats itself. In order to make the most of where I am going in the future, I want to know all I can about my past. I once recorded my grandmother talking about her life through a tape recorder and later through a video camera. In this book, I want to dig deeper into her life and through her own diaries and personal accounts, I want to relive history through her memories that she remembers living over the past one hundred years.

Renee with Mildred on her 80th birthday in 1991

Mildred with Renee on her wedding day in 2008

Chapter 1

A Happy Childhood

Helen Adell Lowry was an excited young girl in 1910. The country was going into the tenth year of the new century and things were changing all around. That January after just welcoming in a new year, she found out she was pregnant with her first child, Mildred Virginia Lowry. Nine months later, on September 30, 1911, the new baby was born.

James Greenway Lowry and Helen were born and raised in the Green Spring Community of Southwest Virginia. Just miles from the town of Abingdon, the life they lived was not that of the city but of a small town or even country living. James was the son of a Confederate soldier, David Lowry, who enlisted in Company K of the 37th Virginia Infantry on April 22, 1861. He transferred to Company D of the 1st Virginia Calvary in December of 1862 through 1864.

David was a Color Bearer at Appomattox Courthouse, and during the surrender, he concealed the flag under his uniform and brought it home with him. He used his flag in local parades and funerals, and displayed it proudly in the parlor of his two story white house in Green Spring. It was this home that Mildred was born in. She still has memories of her grandfather taking all their house guests into the parlor to show off his flag. She never took the kind of interest in it she wishes she had.

Helen was the daughter of David Parks Lowry and Betty Grant Lowry. David was the superintendent of the Washington County School system and a politician. Betty, her mother and a housewife, died at the age of thirty-nine and left Helen's father to raise four children on his own. Both of Mildred's grandfathers were named David Lowry, so to keep free of confusion they called them "Long Dave" and "Short Dave," as one was tall and the other short.

James, known as "Jim," and Helen met as children in the community school and eventually married at a young age in 1909. They had a long honeymoon to Ocala, Florida and on to Savannah, Georgia. Not only was it a honeymoon, but it was also a career venture. Jim worked on the shipping docks in Savannah. It was here that he worked with a black man who called his wife "Love" with an old southern drawl. From then on Helen's nickname was "Love."

Jim worked in Savannah for several months until his parents begged them to return home to the farm. His father promised to give them the house and farm if they would only move back. They did move back by 1911 and lived with James' parents. Mildred Virginia Lowry was born at the end of that September. She was born in that very house where Helen was a homemaker while Jim became, like his father, a farmer. Helen liked the name Mildred, and Virginia was her aunt's middle name. Two years later, Mildred's brother David Horace Lowry was born.

In the early 1900's, raising a family was hard. Country living was much different than living in the city. They lived off the land—what they ate came from crops they planted, when they drank milk it was from cows they milked, and the clothes they wore they made themselves.

The Lowrys, who were from Democratic stock, were well aware through newspapers what was happening in the world. William H. Taft was elected into office in 1908 and began his term in 1909. He was a Republican, and people thought that he would carry on the policies of Theodore Roosevelt. Importantly for James and other farmers in the area, factories, not farms, began to dominate the nation's economy. More Americans were moving to the big cities to work in factories. This was possibly why Jim felt that moving away would be more profitable, but family took first priority.

It wasn't long after Mildred was born that the April 15, 1912 newspaper reported on the sinking of the R.M.S. Titanic. It was taking its maiden voyage from England to New York City on April 14. More than 1,500 lives were lost when the ship hit an iceberg. Three hours later it had sunk into the Atlantic Ocean. A huge controversy in the aftermath of the sinking led to new safety regulations for passenger ships. The Titanic had enough lifeboats to hold 1,178 passengers. There were 2,224 passengers on board that night.

Even though Mildred was just a baby when World War I broke out, it had a lasting effect on the country and on her family, even if it was not direct at the time. On June 28, 1914, Archduke Franz Ferdinand was assassinated in Sarajevo. This led to a chain of events resulting in World War I. Even though President Woodrow Wilson, elected in 1913, stated in 1914 that America would remain neutral, the U.S. entered the war in 1917. The war confused Americans. Even Wilson stated how the war had been caused by nothing in particular. Americans also did not know what side they should take. One hundred million people claimed German decent, a greater number had British ties, and four to five million were Irish Americans. Mildred's ancestors were Scotch-Irish.

When the war was over in 1918, troops came home to an America that was thankfully not torn apart like other countries. However, the map of Europe had changed forever. Shortly after WWI had ended, another type of hardship happened throughout the world and soon came to the little community of Green Spring. 1918 brought the influenza epidemic. Twenty-seven million people perished worldwide, half a million in the United States alone. The last week of October, 1918, 21,000 people died in America alone. Helen made asphidity bags and wrapped them around her children's necks and sent them up to their room to stay next to the stove. She couldn't stand the thought of her family being one of the statistics.

Medicine consisted of home remedies that had been passed down by Helen's parents, and that is how she treated her children. For headaches, she would wrap a belt or towel around their heads as tight as it would go and send them to bed. For cuts and burns, beet juice was poured on the area. When Mildred had a cold, her mother would have her drink onion juice and gargle hot salt water.

An infection some kids had in school that was passed around similar to lice was "the itch." As a treatment, the child was covered in sulfur and then wore hose over arms and legs and set out in the sun to bake. These home remedies were passed on to Mildred who would later use them on her own children.

Growing up on the farm, Mildred did not have to worry about some of the issues that were taking place in the world. Her parents didn't struggle as much as some farmers did, and they were provided with what was needed to live a comfortable life. She played with her rag dolls, dishes, and had tea parties. She also had a playhouse in the old buggy house where they kept their horse drawn buggy.

When school time came, Mildred attended Green Spring Elementary. She would leave out in the winter morning with snow boots laced up high and stockings up to her knees. For lunch her mother would pack her a jelly biscuit. Everyone drank out of the same cistern and they had a cup they would all share. A stove warmed the schoolhouse and the modern day bathroom consisted of a closet size building with a hole in the ground and a wooden seat. This was called the outhouse. The Lowry family did not have indoor plumbing in their house. An outdoor cistern would supply the fresh water, and it was heated on a stove to take baths and cook food.

Electricity came from Aladdin lamps. These lamps were pretty and put out a nice light. Oil would fill the bottoms of the lamp and when one lit the rope that projected from the top, and put the shade on, the light would fill a small room. It wasn't too long after Mildred was born that her father invested in Delco lighting. The 1916 Farm Journal advertised Delco Lighting as the "electricity for every farm." Moving the comforts of the city to the farm, the Delco system was a compact electric plant that would furnish forty to fifty lights per house or barn. It could power not only lamps, but also small appliances such as milkers, washing machines, and churns. The Domestic Engineering Company produced them, and the complete system with batteries ran for $250. This was a luxury for the Lowry family. After Jim installed the system in their machine shed and charged all the batteries, he took the whole family on a walk down the road so they could look back and see their house all lit up.

Mail order catalogs were the best way to shop at the turn of the century. Catalogs from such merchants as the Sears, Roebuck and Company would come in the mail. Mildred and her friend Imogene Garrett would go over to Elizabeth and Frank Kellers house and they would plan out their future houses through the pages of the catalogs. It was their main way of shopping. Newspapers were put out in the town of Abingdon and Bristol. The Green Spring Community had a community paper, which consisted mostly of community events and the gossip of the local families, weddings, births, vacations, and more.

Mildred's mother was a wonderful cook and always had big meals that she and Mildred's grandmother would prepare for the family. Mildred's grandfather raised many vegetables including celery, which they later stored in the spring house. They had an apple house where they stored food during the winter and a meat house where they hung their meat to keep fresh. A regular meal the family ate would consist of fried chicken, potatoes, vegetables, and biscuits. They would also fix boiled ham and beef on occasion. Mildred and her mom would go to the store with $1 and purchase sugar and dried peaches for pies and ice cream.

Jim hired a black family to help him work the farm. They lived in a little house on the hill, which was on the Lowry property. The children of that family were like brothers and sisters to Mildred. She and her brother would play jokes on them as they would each other. One hot summer day Mildred and her brother watched the children carry buckets of water up the hill to their house. They walked behind them throwing rocks in their bucket to make them heavy.

The Lowry family had a telephone since before Mildred was born. The invention of the telephone was first introduced to the world in 1876 at the Philadelphia Centennial Exposition. Alexander Graham Bell had made communication go above and beyond what most thought was magic. It became a form of entertainment for those of the Green Spring Community.

By the turn of the century, over 1.3 million telephones were in service. A favorite saying Mildred had from childhood and remembered the rest of her life was "Hello Central," and the story behind that saying is not one of an event, but one of historical context. Central was a trusted friend, as it referred to the operator on the other end of the line. People would dial up Central and give them the number they wanted them to ring. The Lowry's number was a long and three shorts. The old tune, "Hello Central, Give me Heaven" was based on the concept. The Lowry family was on the Green Spring line and there were six or seven households on one line. They dialed long distance through the operator. The operators in Green Spring were the E.C. Kings. Party lines created gossip in the local community, when one party would listen in on another's conversation.

All Christmases were memorable for Mildred with a Christmas tree and Santa Claus. Not only did Santa come at Christmas, but Kris Kringle came on New Year's and would bring oranges, candy, and nuts. Cracker Jacks became a fun snack in 1896, and was a treat for Mildred along with chewing gum and chocolate bars, which had been invented by Hershey in 1894. However, chocolate and ice cream were rarities. Ice cream was made in the home. Ingredients were expensive, but on special occasions they would walk to the store and purchase them to make ice cream for birthdays or ice cream socials.

The train was the only form of transportation at the turn of the century that allowed a person to travel long distance other than by boat. At the age of nine, Mildred boarded a steam engine train for the first time. She and her mother took a trip to Stephen City, Virginia, to visit her Aunt Eva, her mother's sister. It was a big treat. This way of travel would soon change in the community of Green Spring, when her family along with others would purchase automobiles.

As a child, Mildred along with most children wondered what it would be like to fly like birds. In 1903, the Wright Brothers had shown Americans what it would be like, when they took the first successful flight in an airplane. Airmail resulted from their invention in 1918. It was hard to believe that a machine could actually stay in the clouds.

Most evenings and weekends were filled with social and church events. Helen loved to entertain. Music was very popular in the late teens and early twenties. The only type of music that anyone had to listen to was music you made from a piano, fiddle, or phonograph. Victor Talking Machine Company started the production of phonographs in 1901. They went from a tabletop system to a compact floor model in 1905. The compact phonograph was more convenient for the average household. The horn folded downward into the standing cabinet.

A Victrola phonograph sold for $200, which at the time was too expensive for the average middle class household. By 1911, lower priced models were produced, starting as tabletops and later as floor models. An American family would purchase records to listen to rather than sheet music to play and sing to. This brought entertainment to a whole new level in the 1920's. Most records purchased were operatic and music hall favorites. Many parties the Lowrys had for their children included music. Helen would stand in the hallway next to the family phonograph, cranking it for hours to keep the music going. Mildred's favorite songs were *Let Me Call You Sweetheart*, *Carry Me Back to Old Virginny*, and *I Love You Truly*.

Jim and Helen Lowry in Ocala, Florida
(Mildred's Parents)

David and Etta Keller Lowry
(Mildred's Grandparents)

Lowry House in Green Spring, Virginia

Mildred Virginia Lowry,
born September 30, 1911

Mildred with her new baby brother,
David Horace Lowry

Chapter 2

Love at First Sight

The 1920's brought a whole new way of life in the city, and some of it drifted out to the country. Many social reformers in the nineteenth century objected to the high rate of alcohol consumption. Dry laws were passed which prohibited the manufacture and sale of alcohol. Going much further, the Eighteenth Amendment was passed, which combined with the Volstead Act of 1919, began Prohibition in America. Resources needed to enforce the laws were not available. However, alcohol was still being manufactured in illegal breweries and distilleries. In the mountains of Kentucky and Tennessee, stills were hidden out in the bushes and shacks where "moonshine" was made for local profit. Mildred remembers a family from across the South Holston Lake who were making whiskey in their still. They hid from the law for many years.

During Prohibition came entertainment, especially in the city. The country was booming after the war, and people were living it up. Crossword puzzles, dance marathons, and a self-improvement craze swept the nation. But Mildred was a girl of a country town where this nightlife bootlegging and Mah-jongg playing was unheard of. Her free time was usually spent helping on the farm, playing with friends, or attending church events such as church socials and youth group meetings, which her mother was in charge of. Her father was the superintendent of Sunday school and an elder of Green Spring Church.

In 1921, the Green Spring Church burned. It was a Sunday morning and all the children were in their Sunday school classes having Sunday school. The adult Sunday school classes were going on as well. Ten-year-old Mildred was sitting in her class learning her Bible study when a woman of the church ran in and said the church was on fire. Everyone evacuated the building and men started carrying water to the church. Mildred stood below watching her father climb onto the roof to try and drown out the flames. She hollered for him to be careful, as did all the women standing under the trees praying.

When the fire was over, the church had burned extensively. They had to raise money to rebuild it. Mildred, along with other children in the community, went around to local stores and houses selling cards that people purchased for ten cents. Each card was good for purchasing one shingle. The cornerstone for the present brick church was laid in August of 1923, during the pastorate of Rev. D. H. Graham, and was dedicated in November of 1929 during the pastorate of Rev. J.M. McChesney.

By 1929, nearly twenty-three million automobiles had hit the roadways. With them came road signs, the highway system, and gas stations. It was an easy way to get to town or church, and factory workers would take their families on week long vacations to such places as national parks. It also became a popular way for courtships to move from the parlor to a more private setting. Mildred's Uncle Bob had the first car in the community by 1923. Most folks still walked to church and school, or to the local store. When traveling to Abingdon or Bristol, the horse and buggy was pulled out of the buggy house and the Lowry family would load up in the back.

By the time Mildred was thirteen in 1924, her father Jim had purchased their first car, a Model T Ford. The first production Model T Ford was assembled at the Piquette Avenue Plant in Detroit on October 1, 1908. Over the next nineteen years, Ford would build 15,000,000 automobiles with the Model "T" engine. From 1908-1927, the Model T endured with little change in its design. Mildred can remember traveling in their car with the buttoned curtains and the wind up motor. Many people owned a car before they had indoor plumbing. It became a necessary way of life. The Model T Ford stayed in production until 1927, and cost as little as $290.

One day the family planned a trip to visit some family. Helen had packed a lunch, and Mildred and Dee hopped in the back seat with much excitement. Taking a trip in an automobile was a pleasure and a form of family entertainment. Jim cranked the car to get it started, and off they went down the road. A couple miles down the road their car stopped. Jim got out of the car and checked under the hood. He cranked it over and over and could not get it to start. As his temper raged and he kicked the car, the preacher drove up and asked if they needed help. Mildred saw her father's temper cool quickly, and with the preacher's help the car started and their trip carried on.

Not only had the manufacturing of automobiles taken off, but air travel had passed several milestones. Charles A. Lindbergh became an American Hero when he decided to make the first nonstop flight from New York to Paris. Lindbergh was a pilot flying mail from St. Louis to Chicago. Newspapers were filled with photos and stories of the trip he took on May 20, 1927. He climbed into his single engine monoplane, *The Spirit of St. Louis* in Long Island, New York, and thirty-three hours and twenty-nine minutes later he touched down in Paris. Lindbergh became a household name. Mildred's brother Dee worshiped him. It would always be an unfulfilled dream for Dee to be a pilot.

High School was a fun time for Mildred and her friends. She attended William King High School starting in the eighth grade. It was a city school, which her family thought would provide her with a better education. She moved in with her Aunt Maude Clark, who lived on Valley Street in Abingdon. Her Aunt Maude always took an interest in her. She would buy new clothes for her and take her to parties and shopping. She enjoyed the "city" living and the social life that came along with it. After a year of fun and excitement at William King, she moved back home and attended Cleveland High School for the next three years, not for the education, but for one other important reason... to date her future husband.

Carter Franklin Garrett was a local boy who went to Cleveland High School. His parents Franklin and Musetta Cubine Garrett were well known in the community for owning a lot of farmland. His father was a farmer and his mother was a schoolteacher. When Mildred met Carter, he was singing a solo at school. It was love at first sight when they made eye contact. She fell in love with his dark features and tall stature. From then on she knew all she wanted was to marry Carter and have children.

Along with courting her high school sweetheart, Mildred played basketball with her friends on a girl's league. They wore bloomers as uniforms. It was not proper for girls to wear pants, and when she dressed for a game she would put on her laced up shoes over long stockings and her bloomers that were so baggy they looked like a skirt. When she would jump to make a goal, her pants would fly up and down. She was never a star athlete, and music became her interest.

Mildred took piano lessons, and in school she took voice and expression classes. Music was very important in her family. She sang in the choir at church and took part in many plays and musicals at her school. She never took an interest in academics. She didn't like to read or study. However, she was good in spelling and took several first place awards in spelling bees. She won one contest by spelling the word Czechoslovakia. She always knew she wanted to get married and have a family. Not having a large family herself, she dreamed of a house full of little kids. She also wanted to become a nurse, and let her caring and nurturing skills help others, but her parents didn't want her to.

Along with fun times came mischievous times for Mildred and her friends. Her two closest friends were Mattie Jane "Janie" Jones and Elizabeth Bowman. One sunny afternoon while sitting in the back of class, Mildred and Janie jumped out the back window while the teacher had her back turned. They ran around the schoolhouse and back through the front door where they casually entered the classroom with no notice. Janie's father, Albert Jones, was the principal of the high school, and she and Mildred would often go to his classroom for him to help them with their algebra. While he was trying to help them, they would flirt with the boys in his class.

The roaring Twenties brought a gain in prosperity along with the fear that Americans were producing more goods than were being purchased. This caused great deflation, which would come to the surface in 1929. Agriculture became unprofitable as farmers tried to repay loans they had taken out. Mildred graduated high school in that year. The world would see a great deal of change, and while she went off to college to pursue an education, millions were losing jobs, homes, and sanity.

The Great Depression would be the longest, most widespread and deepest depression of the Twentieth Century. It originated in the U.S., starting with the fall in stock prices that began around September 4, 1929, and became worldwide news with the stock market crash of October 29, 1929, also known as Black Tuesday. It had devastating effects in virtually every country, rich and poor. Unemployment in the U.S. rose to twenty-five percent. Those who had a lot invested in the stock market found themselves selling their cars and homes. Many lost their jobs and even farmers were struggling to sell their crops.

Carter Garrett was a young man who wanted to be a farmer, and after high school he went on to V.P.I., later known as Virginia Tech, to study poultry science. He wanted to breed and raise chickens on his future farm. His time away from home lasted only a couple years. He wanted to move home and marry Mildred who went on to attend Stonewall Jackson College after she graduated from Cleveland in 1929. Stonewall Jackson College was located across the street from the Johnston Memorial Hospital in Abingdon, off of Valley Street. It was later turned into a nursing school. She earned scholarships to go to college, including one scholarship from the Daughters of the American Revolution.

Green Spring Church

Cleveland Grammar School

Harry Jones, Mildred, Carter, and Elizabeth Bowman
at Harry and Janie Jones' home place in May 1927

Mildred and Carter dating

Mildred as a young college student

Carter in his uniform at V.P.I.

Chapter 3

Happiness in a Storehouse

As if the Crash was not bad enough, the Dust Bowl began in 1930 and lasted until 1936. The event was caused by severe drought in the middle states along with decades of extensive farming without techniques to prevent erosion. Drought along with high winds caused clouds of black dust to blow across the country. It led to sickness, and farmers had to move their families from their farms that were no longer able to produce crops. This led to a great migration to California where families were in hopes of better jobs. Many found themselves on a long road to disappointment with deaths along the trail and no jobs available once they arrived. Hoovervilles sprang up in many areas, which were one of many slang terms against the way President Herbert Hoover remained unceasingly optimistic towards the economy. Many of the homeless living in makeshift villages dubbed the term "Hooverville."

The 1930's were a time of poverty and despair for many. Even out in the country where produce was grown in the back yard, other goods such as flour and sugar were rationed at the local store. Fortunately, Mildred's parents invested in land and did not lose money in banks. She did have an uncle who lost everything he owned. That was not an unusual occurrence for one to lose it all. Many women and children across the country looked for jobs. In some parts of the country, especially in the cities, children were on street corners begging for money or selling apples. Drifters started leaving home and moving to find work. A lot of families were torn apart.

Mildred moved back to the town of Abingdon to attend Stonewall Jackson College. She lived with her Aunt Maude with whom she had lived with while going to William King High

School. She was a huge influence on Mildred's life. She would buy her fine clothes to wear and take her to events when Mildred was not studying. Mildred enjoyed being in town where she could meet with friends and attend socials. They had a little ice cream parlor they would meet at to gossip about the school day. Aunt Maude and Mildred would also take trips into Bristol to shop in her two-toned Ford convertible with a rumble seat. It was a sporty car and Mildred found her to be a wild driver.

AUNT MAUDE'S COCONUT CAKE

Box of Duncan Hines White Cake Mix
4 Egg Whites
3 Cups Sugar
1 Cup Hot Water

Mix cake according to directions on box. Divide into two for nine inch pans. Bake according to directions. Remove from oven and cool completely before icing. Icing: Place 3 cups sugar in sauce pan and add 1 cup hot water. Boil together. Beat 4 egg whites until stiff. When sugar and water boil long enough to form string from a spoon, or harden in cold water, pour into beaten egg whites until stiff enough to spread. Use frozen coconut to layer over icing.

The college which Mildred attended was established in 1867. In 1869, the Sinking Spring Presbyterian Church Board of Trustees established the Stonewall Jackson Institute as a female seminary. Its primary purpose along with education was to instill thoroughness, uprightness, and fidelity to duty in its students, which characterized the life of Stonewall Jackson. It not only housed a college, but also primary, intermediate, and high school classes. Annual tuition and board in the early years was about $100. A new campus was constructed after a 1914 fire destroyed the old buildings. It was this campus that Mildred attended until

1930, when the college closed due to financial losses.

Mildred transferred to Martha Washington College in 1930 and attended there until 1931. The college was the former home of the Preston Family, who sold the mansion for $21,000 in 1858. In 1860, it became an upscale college for young women. The school was named Martha Washington College, in honor of the first First Lady, but was called "The Martha" by locals. The Civil War had an effect on the schoolgirls who became nurses as the grounds had become training barracks for the Washington Mounted Rifles. The college also served as a makeshift hospital for the wounded, both Confederate and Union soldiers. The college was advertised as having steam heating and lighting by incandescent electric lights. It had over 350 graduates from many states. By 1931, the Great Depression, typhoid fever, and declining enrollment had taken its toll on the college, and it closed in 1932.

Mildred had some good times in college, not just with friends, but also at her Aunt Maude's. She can remember one day a salesman came to the house selling player pianos. He left one for Mildred and her aunt to play on for several months. She enjoyed playing the piano and singing in college. She majored in voice and piano.

One of the most exciting experiences Mildred had in College was when she and her glee club traveled to Knoxville to broadcast. Mrs. Cline, wife of a local doctor, sponsored the club and took them to sing in front of the mic for those in radio world to hear. It was a huge event. In the 1930's radio had really taken off and broadcasts being heard included not only music and news, but also variety shows, dramas, and comedies. Broadcast radio began in 1915 when speech was first transmitted across the country from New York City to San Francisco. The 1930's to the 1950's were called the "Golden Age" of radio.

There were several college parties that stood out as embarrassing moments in Mildred's mind. Being a country girl and being raised around a loving family, Mildred knew manners and always tried to be on her best behavior at social functions. She always told herself that there was a time for being mischievous and having fun, and a time to put on airs and be dignified and aristocratic. These parties were the times she told herself to fit in and be dignified.

One Saturday afternoon, Dr. Frank Smith and his wife hosted a party at their house for the Stonewall girls. The maids would come out to serve them at the long dining room table that was all fixed up with flowers and fine china. After dinner, the maids brought out dessert. A delicious cupcake was set in front of Mildred with decadent icing. Mildred picked it up and started eating it. The first bite was delicious, and so was the second bite. After taking the third bite, she felt a hair pull out of the moist cake and into her mouth. She did not want to be rude and pull it out and surely didn't want to draw attention to it and embarrass the maid. With that thought in mind, she shoved the rest of the cupcake in her mouth along with the hair, and swallowed.

Mildred and Carter attended a party at a friend's house while she was attending Martha Washington. They served hors d'oeuvres and wine before the meal. Mildred had not eaten anything, and her empty growling stomach gave way to nausea after she drank a couple glasses of wine. After two glasses, she started feeling woozy and Carter had to take her out driving for a while before dinner. She saw another man sitting in the corner who had too much as well. She had never drunk wine before and did not know the effects until that night. It turned her from it the rest of her days!

Cities had ways to entertain people to get their minds off the depression, and authors and directors were playing off the depression to write new books and produce new movies. Silent films that Mildred remembered from her young life were now being put to sound, and you could hear what the actors and actresses were saying on the big screen. It was called the "Silver Screen," due to the screens reflective quality. In the 1930's, movie theaters were the place to be. *Wizard of Oz* and *Snow White* were some of the family favorites.

It was in Abingdon and Bristol where Carter and Mildred courted. They would go to plays at the Barter Theatre and films at the Paramount Theatre in Bristol. Carter drove his family's new Chevrolet. It was a tan sedan. They also double dated with Carter's brother Claude and his girlfriend Bernice. He drove a Ford that had a rumble seat on the back where Carter and Mildred would sit.

They would go on dates to church socials and to Sunday school. Dating in the thirties mostly consisted of socializing with groups of friends in their homes. They would have ice cream socials, dances, bacon bats, and weenie roasts. A lot of these parties would last long into the evening after dark.

The Paramount Theatre in Bristol, Tennessee, opened on February 20, 1931 with the film *It Pays to Advertise*. The show and theater was a huge hit. They had to turn hundreds of people away. The theater was the seventh theater in America that was built acoustically for "sound movies." People were used to watching silent films, and to watch a movie and hear what the actors were saying was an amazing attraction.

When going to Bristol to watch a film, Mildred and Carter would take his family's automobile and park downtown. They would walk to The Sweet Shop across the street to get their snacks before the movie. To see a movie at night, it cost fifty cents, thirty-five cents for matinees and children got in for ten cents. It was especially nice to see a movie in the summer time since the Paramount was the first in the region to have "refrigerated air." We know it today as air conditioning.

> *"Pauline, Uncle Eugene and I went down to Aunt Joe's for dinner. Came back home about 4 o'clock and we went down to Aunt Bess's for supper. Came home about 8 o'clock. Carter took Pauline and I to Bristol to the show "Frankenstein." We got home about 12:30. A big time – All day."*
>
> —Saturday, Feb. 13, 1932

In 1931 after the Martha Washington College ended its school year and was soon to close, Mildred moved back home with her parents in Green Spring. She spent her time preparing to marry her high school sweetheart who had proposed to her on Nov. 14, 1931 at Hooks Infirmary. Mildred had her tonsils removed the day before, and was recovering when Carter brought her diamond to her. When they told her parents the good news, her father replied, "Well, we sure are gonna miss little sis." She promised her parents that she would go to church and Sunday school every week after she married.

In the following months, Mildred helped her mother and grandmother at home. She went to quilting parties, visited family and friends almost every afternoon, and cooked and cleaned. Her future husband was working on the farm and raising his chickens. They continued to court by going out to socials and the Christian Endeavors at church. Carter was a member of the Cleveland Presbyterian Church, where he and Mildred would soon start attending as a couple.

> *"(Carter's Birthday) Mama and I went down to Aunt Eva's to help quilting. We had a good time. Carter phoned he couldn't come tonight he was water bound. I wrote to Eva King tonight."*
>
> —Wednesday, Feb. 3, 1932

> *"We ironed this morning. Slept this p.m. Oh, what a rainy gloomy day. We heard tonight that the Lindberg baby had been found dead near it's home. A terrible thing."*
>
> —Thursday, May 12, 1932.

It was the crime of the century. In 1930, Charles Lindbergh and his new bride had a baby, Charles Jr. His birth was front-page news everywhere, but the family shunned all publicity and shielded themselves from prying eyes by retreating to a new home.

On the night of March 1, 1932, Charles Jr. caught a cold. His nursemaid sewed him a flannel nightshirt, tucked him into a crib and let him sleep. At 10 p.m., she went upstairs to check on him. The crib was empty. Investigators found a ransom note demanding $50,000. Unfortunately, after paying the ransom, Lindberg received the dreaded news. On May 12, a truck driver found the baby just four miles from the Lindbergh home. A coroner identified the body as Charles Lindbergh Jr.

On May 31, 1932, Mildred and five friends went to Sarasota, Florida, in a school bus that her cousin Doc Bowman drove. For the trip, he turned it into a sleeper bus with curtains and sheets, which made partitions for the men and women. When they neared the Gulf of Mexico, Mildred's friend Bill said, "Look Mildred, it's the ocean." It was really a lake. A few miles after being fooled by her friends, Mildred saw the real ocean for the first time in her life. It was a natural wonder that amazed her. While in Florida, they all stayed at Lowrey Bowman's house. He had moved to Florida to become a preacher.

> *"Cousin Doc, Bill, Mr. Watt Gray, Margaret, Vivian and I left for Sarasota, Fla. at 6:30, Tues., May 31. Traveled all-night and got to Lowrey's at 10:30 Wed. night. Had a grand time while there. We stayed until Tues., June 7. Left Sarasota about 1:30. Spent Tues. night near Ocala, Fla. near Silver Springs. Spent next night near Augusta, Ga. Arrived home Thurs. night about 11:30. I sure had a grand time."*
>
> —Thursday, June 9, 1932

The Depression caused a downswing in lumbering, the trend that had boosted the prosperity of the area after the Civil War. The depression closed the Martha Washington College; however, one of Abingdon's greatest treasures was established during the rough times, bringing laughter and entertainment to many in the community.

The Barter Theatre opened in 1933. The building had previously been the Sinking Spring Presbyterian Church, started in 1832. During the twenties and Prohibition, it became "Temperance Hall." Offices were housed in the building and the jail was located in the basement.

Robert Porterfield turned the building into the Barter Theatre when he gathered twenty-two fellow actors and headed to Abingdon, located near his hometown of Glade Spring, Virginia. He established the idea of "ham for Hamlet," bartering food and produce in exchange for a ticket to the theater, hence the name Barter Theatre. Playwrights for the theater have included Noel Coward, Tennessee Williams, George Bernard Shaw and Thornton Wilder. Many famous voices were heard coming from the stage, including Ernest Borgnine, Hume Cronyn, Gregory Peck, and Ned Beatty. Mildred went to the Barter often and so did her mother and Aunt Bess. They would take a chicken and eggs for barter.

Some marriages in the 1930's were put on hold due to the depression. Elaborate weddings were unheard of at the time, and getting married mostly consisted of driving to the nearest Justice of the Peace or preacher's house and saying your vows.

On February 22, 1933, Mildred and Carter were married at the Green Spring Manse. Only a few friends and family attended the ceremony. Afterwards, the new couple left in their automobile, which was chased over the hill by a crowd of friends. Carter cut through the field at the high school to lose them. They had cans and ribbons flying out the back of his automobile. They attended a play at the Paramount Theatre in Bristol and then returned to Mildred's Aunt Maude's house in Abingdon for the night. At midnight, the couple awoke to a chivalry. It was a ritual to gather a group of friends and visit the newlyweds after they had gone to bed. The group would shoot guns, bang pots and pans, and sing.

Mildred and Carter lived with Carter's parents until he

refinished an old storehouse. It was above the old Garrett Mercantile, which had been run by one of Carter's cousins. When Carter purchased the storehouse, a feed house was located downstairs. Carter bought the upstairs house and turned it into a fine home. He built new cabinets and put fresh paint on the walls. They furnished it with some pieces belonging to their families and Carter built a new corner cabinet with glass doors. Mildred was as happy in that storehouse as she would have been in a newly built mansion. She cooked and sewed.

Carter worked on his farm and built his chicken coops to raise chickens. His father had divided up all his land and gave the boys their pick of either land or money. Carter chose the land around the storehouse, and the acres extending out to where their future house would be built. Carter worked the farm and also did carpentry work. He built several houses and remodeled churches and local buildings.

Mildred missed her family during the first year of marriage. There were several occasions that she cried to go home and Carter took her for a few days. She loved her home, but loved Carter more, and was always happy being in the storehouse with him.

In March 1933, Mildred became pregnant with her first child. It was hard planning for a family in the years of the depression.

Having a talent or being a farmer helped those in the country. The world was still suffering through the depression. Mildred made her clothes at home and would sew new shirts for Carter. When she went to the store, she noticed sugar and flour were sold in smaller quantities due to rising prices of goods.

The rolling store also came through the community. It was an easier way of purchasing goods rather than having to drive into town. A rolling store consisted of a store in an automobile, usually a truck with a large covered bed. When Mildred was a child, it was a horse drawn wagon. It was stocked with bread, flour, household items, and some clothes and hats. Anything a regular store would have, the truck driver stocked up on. Mildred's cousin, Doc

Bowman, drove the rolling store in the Green Spring Community.

Mildred and Carter kept their faith through the depression, and started a family. On December 24, 1933, Mildred was taken to Fleenor's Hospital in Bristol and gave birth to a new baby boy, Carter Frank Garrett Jr. He was an "instrument baby," which meant they used an instrument to pull him out. Today they are called forceps. He had small indentions in his head for a while, but was a normal and healthy baby. The nurse cleaned him up and laid him in a drawer from a chest of drawers in Mildred's room. Mildred and her first born listened to the bells ringing in Christmas from the church across the street.

One day while in the storehouse, Mildred looked out her window and saw a string of gypsies riding down the road. Gypsies were known in those days as being beggars and robbers. She ran downstairs and brought in her dog and locked the doors. She feared for the safety of her baby. The gypsies rode through on their horses and in their wagons. Dressed in long skirts and traveling with several dogs, the long gypsy train passed by her, and went on to her father in law's house. When Mr. Garrett stood talking to them, one stole his wallet. They moved on without anyone getting hurt.

At the end of September 1934, Mildred found out she was pregnant with her second child. James "Jimmy" Lowry Garrett was born June 29, 1935. He was also born at Fleenor's Hospital in Bristol. Carter had not shaved the morning he took Mildred to the hospital. After the delivery, the nurse said to Mildred she had another baby boy. Mildred looked up at her and said, "Well, is he shaved?"

It was hard taking care of two babies. Mildred had never been around children or had to take care of them, so having two of her own was quite the challenge. She had the support and help of her family who were at their house regularly to help.

The family was getting larger and Carter and Mildred were ready to build their home in the community of Cleveland. The

Rutherford Brothers along with Carter built a new two-story white house. They painted the shutters black and built a big porch across the front. It was close to their families and their church where they both remained very active. The house was finished in 1937, just in time for their third son to be born.

David Eugene "Gene" Garrett was born on September 7, 1937. Gene was born at home. It was a very messy and rainy evening and the roads were beginning to flood. Mildred's sister-in-law Bernice came over to the house to help out. When the baby was ready to be born, they called Dr. Wolf to come. The doctor got lost in the flood and Bernice delivered the baby by herself. At Carter's parent's house, his mother was getting ready to go to Mildred and Carter's house to help out with the big event. She was all excited due to the storm, flood, and her third grandchild being born. She was a large lady. She was stern to some and yet a gentle and kind lady. She was so excited and in a hurry, that she fell down her steps on her way to see the baby. When she got to Mildred's, she sat in a corner ashamed and stove up from the fall.

After Gene was born, and the family had moved into their new house, Carter's half sister Blanche phoned that she needed a home for two orphaned children. Blanche was a well-traveled lady who never married. She was a missionary who had lived in Florida, North Carolina, and West Virginia. She opened an orphanage in Big Stone Gap. In 1937 she decided it was time to close the orphanage. She had all the children put in homes or found families to adopt them. She had two last children who she loved dearly. They were older, and needed a family to stay with while getting through high school. Their names were Oma and Bobby Austin. Mildred and Carter agreed to take Oma if Blanche would help clothe her.

Oma was a huge help to Mildred who was busy with three small children and another on the way. Oma's brother Bobby lived with several families in the community including Mildred and Carter for a short while. He went on to work and marry. Oma graduated while with Mildred and went on to become a nurse and marry Harold Hall, Mildred's first cousin. They had six children: Charles, Lowry, Sandra, Ricky, Barbara, and Karen.

Mildred always knew she wanted a large family. She already had three boys and was ready for a little girl. Patty Sue Garrett was born on December 8, 1938. She was also born at home. During this pregnancy, Mildred wore an old pair of white shoes that were dirty and old yet the most comfortable pair she had and did not want to get rid of them. She promised her mother that she would burn them after she gave birth. That was the first thing the family did after Patty was born. They took her shoes and threw them in the fireplace. They were all excited to have a girl. Visitors came for days to see the Garrett's first baby girl.

Having four young children was a pleasure, but also a lot of hard work. Just getting ready to go to church on Sunday mornings was a difficult task. Still, children hardly ever missed a Sunday. Mildred would wake up early in the morning and fix a big breakfast and start lunch. After getting the children dressed, they would all sit on the couch and Carter would shine their shoes and fix their hair. One Sunday morning they all walked in to a full Cleveland Church and walked up to a front side pew. Mr. Bill Bowman looked over at Mildred who was carrying baby Patty. He pointed at the growing Garrett family, trying to embarrass Mildred, and counted one... two... three... four... and shook his head.

The Martha Washington Inn
in Abingdon, Va

The new Garrett home Carter
built for his growing family

Aunt Maude outside her
house in Abingdon

Cleveland Presbyterian Church

Chapter 4

"We're Happy in My Blue Heaven"

It took a while for those hit hard by the depression to get ahead again, but for the lucky ones the worst was over. World War II was the event that changed the decade from a poor and frustrated country to an industrial and productive one. The depression years were finally over.

European artists and intellectuals came to the U.S. to escape Hitler and the Holocaust. Our country may have been getting back to normal, but for other countries, turmoil that they experienced was nothing that the U.S. had ever known.

Franklin D. Roosevelt was president until 1945. He led American troops into war while General Dwight Eisenhower commanded troops in Europe. So much was going on in the world, and wives and parents had prayed that the U.S. would not get involved. Hitler invaded Poland bringing France and Great Britain into the war. Japan took over Manchuria bringing China into the war. Germany invaded the USSR bringing the Soviet Union into the war.

The Garrett family enjoyed a simple life on the farm. Little did they know what the world was getting ready to experience. The day before Patty's third birthday, on December 7, 1941, the Japanese attacked a U.S. fleet at Pearl Harbor, bringing America into World War II.

Americans were now going through another hard time. Most men were drafted into war and women found themselves on the home front taking over. Families were once again torn apart by war and World War II would be an event that would not only change America's economy, but also its way of thinking.

The government reclassified fifty-five percent of all jobs. Women and blacks were being hired to do what only white men had done in years past. The role of women was redefined, going from homemaker to breadwinner. Many began working in factories doing production work for the war. In the country, women whose husbands went off to war had to take over the farm. Roughly half of all women in the U.S. were working outside the home. Rosie the Riveter was a figure seen on war effort posters that symbolized the working woman. The whole country worked towards the war effort, from working in production lines and assembling weapons, to sewing parachutes.

The 1940's began another time of savings for families. People were regaining money from the depression, but rationing for war was now limiting the supply of goods they could purchase. The federal government set up a rationing system in 1942 that limited the purchase of sugar, coffee, meat, fish, butter, eggs, cheese, shoes, rubber, and gasoline. Silk and newly invented nylon was used to produce parachutes, and so women around the world found it hard to get fashion stockings.

Even though events around the world were being broadcast on radio, and families around the country stayed close to hear what was happening next, the Garrett family went on with their every day lives. Mildred's boys were too young to worry about being drafted and Carter was too old. They escaped the front lines of battle, but still, Americans were fighting the war on "the home front."

Farm production was vital to the war effort, so farmers received extra rations of gasoline and other supplies. It was hard to get new machinery, as factories were retooled to produce tanks rather than tractors. Many farms were using tractors to make farming easier for women while their men were off to war.

As far as family rationing, each member of the household got a ration booklet, usually distributed at the local school. Each booklet had stamps in it that translated into a certain amount of the commodity being rationed. There were only enough stamps for one person to buy 28 ounces of meat per week. Merchants collected the stamps when you bought your items, and after your stamps for that item were gone for the week, no more items could be purchased.

The rationing once again put a strain on the family of six, but they had plenty of freshly grown vegetables and animals, which provided them with fresh meat, eggs, and milk.

Holidays were still made special, especially Christmas. Santa Claus always treated the children nicely. They would put up a Christmas tree in the living room and decorate it with ornaments and hand-made decorations. Several new toys were put on the market in the 1930's and 40's. Monopoly and Scrabble were board games that families enjoyed. During the war, toys were being mass produced and new board games such as Candy Land and Chutes and Ladders were produced. Families enjoyed simple, inexpensive fun. Silly Putty was discovered by a General Electric Engineer who was trying to create a synthetic rubber for war efforts and ended up creating a fun stretchy and bouncy toy that went on the market in the forties.

Instead of stockings, Mildred and Carter fixed up shoe boxes and filled them with apples, oranges, pencils, and a little candy to give their children. A huge Christmas dinner was fixed, and all the family came over to Mildred's house. She always had a homemade applesauce cake for dessert.

APPLESAUCE CAKE

2 ½ Cup Hot Applesauce
4 Tsp. Soda
1 Cup Butter
2 Cups Brown Sugar
1 Egg
4 Cups Flour
1 Tsp. Cinnamon
1 Tsp. Allspice

Add 4 tsp. Soda to the 2 ½ cup hot applesauce. Let cool. Cream butter and brown sugar. Add 1 egg, 4 cups flour, cinnamon and allspice. Add the applesauce. Mix well. To mixture, add 3 cups raisins, chopped dates, fruit cake mix, strawberry preserves, lots of walnuts and anything you desire. Bake 350 degrees for 1 hour or 1 ¼ hour. Cool in pan-1 hour. I freeze this.

In the spring and summer, the boys enjoyed playing out in the fields and helping out on the farm. Patty played with her brothers, who often teased her as brothers do.

Once again, music and movies were dominating the world of entertainment as many spent money on them to get their minds off of world affairs. The Big Band era produced many popular names that performed "swing" music. Glenn Miller, Benny Goodman, Perry Como, and Frank Sinatra were big names heard on the radio. Men who traveled home on R and R enjoyed taking their girlfriends to dance halls and movie theaters. The radio was the lifeline for Americans. Comedians like Red Skelton and Bob Hope gave humor to evening news reports heard at home.

Hollywood directors began making Signal Corps documentaries or training films to aid the war effort, such as *Why We Fight*, which was released from 1942 until 1945. These films hit the hearts of many boys who saw them, and who would later decide to enlist. It also gave others in America such as mothers of soldiers, a better perspective of war and backed up why we were in war, which some thought to be a waste.

Farm life was busy with four children to raise, meals to prepare, and social events to attend. A huge event in the summer was threshing. Winter wheat was planted in the fall and ready to harvest in the summer. Threshing crews would come through once a year with big threshing machines that separated the stalks from the kernels. The stalks, called straw, was used for bedding and the food of animals. The kernels were turned into grain to take to market.

Not only was this a job for the men, but women gathered to prepare large meals to feed the crews. Mildred remembers working for days to prepare a meal for the fifteen to twenty workers. One day the crew worked so late that supper was served at 11 p.m. The meal was never complete without Mildred's homemade rolls.

REFRIGERATOR ROLLS

1 Yeast Cake
1 ½ Tbs. Crisco
¼ Tsp. Salt
1 Cup Lukewarm Water
¼ Cup Sugar
1 Egg White (Beaten)

Combine yeast, sugar and salt into mixing bowl. Pour warm water over this. Let stand 20 minutes. Add 1 beaten egg white and some flour and beat. Add warm shortening. Keep adding flour and beat until soft dough. Knead well and set aside until double its size. Work dough down and place in refrigerator until chilled. Remove. Roll out and make into rolls. Let rise in warm place until dough doubles. Bake at 450 degrees. You can double this.

Carter's parents had "tenants" that worked their farm with them. One of the tenants was using the outhouse next to the creek. While the father was using the outhouse, his son walked up and tipped it over into the creek. When the father asked what happened, his son said, "I don't know." After his father and mother confronted him, he confessed that he turned it over. He added however that George Washington cut down a cherry tree when he was a boy. His mother looked at him and said, "Yes, but his father wasn't sitting in the cherry tree was he?"

On August 6, 1945, the U.S. dropped the first atomic bomb on Hiroshima. Three days later another atomic bomb was dropped on Nagasaki. On September 2, 1945, people listened attentively as they heard of Japan's surrender, and World War II was over. The country along with the whole world celebrated the end of the war and the arrival home of troops. Parades were held, and soldiers came home as heroes.

It wasn't until after the war was over that Americans heard more of the Holocaust and all that happened in Europe during the war. This time in European history was full of fear and hardship for European Jews. The Holocaust was the genocide of approximately six million European Jews during World War II. Throughout Nazi Germany, extermination camps were set up where Jews were taken and eventually killed after harsh treatment, starvation, and abuse. Approximately two-thirds of the population of nine million Jews who had resided in Europe before the Holocaust perished. However, if you include all the other groups such as homosexuals, gypsies, people with disabilities, and others who were killed by the Nazis, the death total would have been between 11 million and 17 million people.

Adolf Hitler was the leader of the Nazi Party. He was the Chancellor of Germany from 1933 to 1945. Hitler is most known for his central leadership role in the rise of fascism in Europe before and during World War II. People in America would hear him give speeches on the radio and shiver at the hatred in his foreign voice. He wanted his nation and armies to be perfect. Anyone who did not live up to his "normal" standards were persecuted. Stories started to emerge from Europe, and Americans wondered why they had not done more to help.

After World War II, Americans saw economic growth and prosperity. This time was dubbed "The Baby Boom Era." The G.I. Bill of Rights was created for returning veterans. It provided them with college or vocational training, as well as one year of unemployment compensation. It also provided many different types of loans for returning veterans to buy homes and start businesses. Along with it came a whole new commercialized way of life for the men and their families. Men who had gotten engaged or married before the war returned home to start new lives with their wives. "The Baby Boom" phrase came from the huge increase in birth rate after the war. Those who already had babies were having one or two more, and others who were starting a family could plan on financially providing for a larger family.

In 1947, America entered a different kind of war. Men were not sent overseas to fight until the Korean War, but a political and military conflict broke out between communist countries, such as the Soviet Union and its independent states and allies, and the Western World including the United States. It wasn't direct fighting, but they expressed conflict through military coalitions, espionage, propaganda, and nuclear arms races. Sports rivalry would emerge along with technological competition and the Space Race. Over the next thirty plus years, this would be known as the Cold War.

The Garrett boys were now in school. Patty was learning how to help around the house and cook. They always goofed around with each other, and the boys would wrestle with their dad in the hallway. Carter Jr. was feeling like he was a man at fourteen years old and the oldest son; however, he had the worst whipping in his life when his uncle caught him smoking under a tree between the Garrett's house and the store. He had gone to the store with twenty-five cents and purchased cigarettes and a bar of candy. He had never experimented with cigarettes, and after he lit up the first one, here came his uncle. His dad found out about it and Carter Jr.'s rear end stayed red for weeks.

County fairs were always a big event in the spring and summer. The boys would enter their sheep and cattle in contests. Women had baking contests and craft contests, showing off quilts and needle point work. The 4-H Club that the boys were members of put on demonstrations. It was a time for the community to all come together and enjoy the fellowship.

In 1948, the South Holston Lake was built just across the road from the Garrett home. It was a large attraction for people to see. The family would often sit on their front porch and watch it being built. Many people had to sell off land to allow the lake to run through. Some even lost their homes. Carter's two-story home place was moved from the new lake location to the top of the hill. Fortunately, Mildred and her family remained in their home without losing it or their land. They even had a pretty sight to see from their porch after the project was completed.

At the end of the 1940's, Mildred was surprised to find out she was pregnant. She worried about the baby and herself, being thirty-seven years old at the time and ten years after her last child was born. With the new decade approaching, more inventions were invented to make a housewife's life a little easier. Mildred went visiting one afternoon while Carter and the boys stayed behind and canned beans for her. When she returned, Carter said, "If you don't want a new oven, I do." He had such a hard time working with their wood stove, that he went out and purchased a new electric oven and installed it in their kitchen in 1948.

In that same year, Carter purchased a school bus to run for the Washington County School System. Carter Jr. gave his dad the idea when he heard his bus driver, Paul Barrett, say that he was going to sell his bus. Paul's wife's name was Lucy, and they had driven school buses for years. After Carter purchased his bus, he gave Mildred the nickname "Lucy," and it stuck for years to come. Carter ran the bus through the areas of Cleveland, Green Spring, and Mock Knob. He transported children to Cleveland Elementary and High School.

On September 10, 1948, Linda Kay Garrett was born at Johnston Memorial Hospital. She was stubborn being born. Mildred took a pain at home and went to the hospital. She can remember being in the room and a large nurse coming in and telling her she needed to have an enema. Afterwards, the nurse looked at Mildred and said, "I don't know if you are having a baby, or just a bowel movement!"

Carter had Mildred and the new baby brought home in an

ambulance. The whole family was excited, especially Patty who had been raised with all boys. She now had a baby sister. At age ten, she was able to help out her mother with the new baby and around the house.

Lowry Family Reunion 1940 (Mildred and Carter –far right)

Mildred with Linda, born September 1948

Patty, Gene, Jimmy, and Carter Jr.

Chapter 5

Living on Love

The 1950's were a busy and prosperous time for families. In Mildred's diaries she describes the activities of the day. And every day was full of something, from cleaning and cooking, to raising kids and taking care of her parents. The family visited friends and family in the evenings, and attended church events on the weekends.

The radio had been replaced with the television, which families surrounded in the evenings to watch the news, soap operas, and cartoons. Television made its debut at the 1939 World's Fair, but the war had stalled production. In 1947, commercial "TV" with thirteen stations became available to the public. This introduced a whole new way of advertising. With the radio, people only heard of new products. With the television, people could sit in the comfort of home and see the products come to life on a screen. It made things more tangible, and with the economy booming, America became a consumer society.

The Garrett family bought their first television in the fifties and set it in their living room. Mildred thought it was more entertaining because now you could not only hear characters talking, but you could see them as well. It made everything in the country more tangible to the public. Not only did you hear how pretty something was on a commercial, but now you could see the item on the television and it made you want it even more. The world of commercialism boomed.

Politics also changed through television. Now Americans could see their candidates on television, along with seeing how they dressed and their mannerisms.

In the news, journalists reported on the big events of the fifties such as the Warsaw Pact, NATO, Space Race, and the threat of nuclear war. These were big worries to the leaders of the country and to President Harry S. Truman who was sworn in after President Roosevelt's death in 1945. Roosevelt was the only president who had been elected for more than two terms, and when he died, an editorial in *The New York Times* declared, "Men will thank God on their knees a hundred years from now that Franklin D. Roosevelt was in the White House."

The Cold War was escalating, and in 1950, the Soviet-aided army of North Korea invaded South Korea, starting the Korean War. Americans would later call this the Forgotten War, since many of the issues were less clear than past conflicts such as World War II. This war started by military conflict between the Republic of Korea, supported by the United Nations, and North Korea, supported by the People's Republic of China. The Soviet Union provided military material aid. There had been a physical division of Korea since the end of World War II. President Harry Truman later wrote this in his autobiography:

> *"Communism was acting in Korea, just as Hitler, Mussolini, and the Japanese had ten, fifteen, and twenty years earlier. I felt certain that if South Korea was allowed to fall, Communist leaders would be emboldened to override nations closer to our own shores. If the Communists were permitted to force their way into the Republic of Korea without opposition from the free world, no small nation would have the courage to resist threat and aggression by stronger Communist neighbors."*
>
> —Harry S. Truman

National fear was calmed a little by the new layout of housing, pulling communities together to socialize and lift each other up. The development of suburbs created the sense of community away from the city, and children rode their bikes down the streets and played baseball in the yard. A summer's night was filled with cookouts and lawn parties, and the women stayed home with their pearls and aprons fixing dinner for their executive husbands.

In the country, family get-togethers happened more often and usually occurred on Sunday afternoons. Mildred would get up early before church to start the meal. Not only did Mildred's parents come over, but all the family including aunts, uncles, cousins, children, and grandchildren all gathered under one roof to talk, laugh, and spend time together. After a huge meal, the family would sit on the porch or play croquet in the yard.

POTATO SALAD

6 Potatoes- Peeled, Cubed and Cooked
¾ Onion- Chopped
2 Eggs- Cooked and Chopped
1 Cup Chopped Celery (optional)
Pickles
Pepper Relish
Mustard
Mayonnaise
Salt

Cook potatoes after cubing and put in refrigerator to chill overnight. Remove and add chopped onion, eggs, celery and pickle. Add a pinch of salt and pickle juice to taste. Add mayonnaise and mustard to taste. Stir all together. Some pepper relish may add color and taste. You can add too or take from anything you don't like.

Many new appliances came out for housewives in the 1950's. The old way of doing things by hand was being replaced by electric appliances. Television would play these items up as being impossible to live without, and the housewife could see them being demonstrated on screen.

The old way to wash clothes was to hand wash them in a tub with a washboard and then run them through a ringer. Aside from the early wringer/washer machine, washing and drying machines were not combined until the latter half of the twentieth century, when the fully electric versions of the machines were better perfected. General Electric produced an electric washer and dryer in 1947, and also invented the first washer dryer combination unit in 1954. Mildred used each of these in her home. Her washer/dryer combo put out by Bowman Grey was not as efficient and was later replaced by separate units.

The 1950's kitchen had replaced the 1930's kitchen that Mildred remembered her mother having. Changes such as new materials, gadgetry, and electric appliances had changed the modern housewife's time spent in the kitchen. In 1951, Mass Observation Study found that the average housewife worked seventy-five hours a week, spending about a quarter of that time in the kitchen. Mass production and the end of rationing in 1954 made refrigerators, vacuum cleaners, coffee makers, food mixers, stainless steel sinks, and all other new appliances more accessible.

Mildred had kept diaries through her younger years, but through school they got misplaced and were not kept up as much as they were in the 1950's. Several excerpts from her diaries share the daily events of her family life in the early 1950's.

> *"Carter took me to Bristol at 1 o'clock to vanity shop to get permanent. Got through at 4 o'clock. Cost $10.00. Carter came after me after school."*
>
> —Tuesday, June 29, 1951

> *"A salesman came with sewing machines. Carter bought Patty one. $189.00, $60.00 for old one."*
>
> —Friday, April 18, 1952

> *"Cleaned house. Made cake for circle. Election Day. Eisenhower elected President."*
>
> —Tuesday, Nov. 4, 1952

Mildred was a member of the Home Demonstration Club where she and other women got together and taught and learned how to cook, sew, quilt, etc. They would eat dessert or have luncheons and socialize through the afternoon. This along with church activities, school events, and church circle groups kept her very busy. She was the treasurer of the PTA, and very active in the kids school activities. There was not a lot of time for extra activity.

The drive-in theater was a popular destination that they tried to make time for. The drive-in theater was the creation of Richard M. Hollingshead, Jr. In 1932 he conducted outdoor theater tests in his driveway with a screen nailed to two trees, a 1928 Kodak projector on the hood of his car, and a radio behind the screen. He was given a patent in 1933 for his invention, and his first drive-in opened in New Jersey the same year. It caught on in several other states, which opened auto parks and drive-in theaters throughout the late 1930's.

In the 1950's, drive-ins peaked in popularity. Families could take care of babies while watching a movie in the privacy of their car. Most drive-ins had playgrounds children could play on, and teenagers found the drive-in to be the perfect date destination.

"Ironed. Tonight we all went to Moonlite to show "Lum and Abner." Enjoyed it lots."

—Wednesday, July 18, 1951

"Did large wash. Carter, Patty, Gene, Linda and I went to Moonlite- "Jumpin Jacks" was real good. Army Life."

—Monday, June 14, 1952

The Moonlite in Abingdon and the Beacon in Bristol were two popular drive-in theaters that the family would go to or where the boys would take their dates. All three boys were dating in the 1950's. Carter Jr. met Donna Marie Talley and they dated through high school. Gene dated in high school for a short time until he met Agnes Weatherly, a basketball player for Valley Institute, with whom he fell in love with at an early age. Jimmy dated several girls, but enjoyed racing his car and hanging out with friends just as much.

A night Mildred never forgot was when Jimmy was out after dark with his cousin Lee, and they had a wreck in Bristol. It was a pretty serious wreck, breaking Jimmy's nose and banging them up pretty badly. Mildred stayed up waiting on him to get home as she did all the children. A hearse pulled up to the house and a man from the funeral home knocked on the door. He had brought Jimmy home from the wreck. The car was totaled, but both boys lived to tell about it.

The family stayed busy with the farm and the other two business ventures that came in the fifties. Carter Jr. became the youngest bus driver in the county. He got permission from the superintendent to drive his dad's school bus at the age of fifteen.

He would drive the bus with Donna Marie sitting next to him on the heater. He always stopped by the store to buy an Orange Crush and a pack of peanuts. He would pour the peanuts into his drink for a tasty beverage. In the 1950's you could buy an eight-inch candy bar or a pack of crackers (called nabs in those days) for a nickel.

Jimmy, also being a young boy, drove the bus and was so short he had to turn the seat over to see out the window. Carter later hired Howard Poe to drive one bus, after they bought a brand new one. The family drove to Indiana to pick it up. This was Mildred's first stay in a motel, which she enjoyed greatly. Linda bounced up and down the aisle in the new bus as they drove it home. From 1952 until 1957, the Garrett family ran three school buses for the county. Children enjoyed Carter driving. He would stop at the local grocery store and let them off to get a drink or ice cream after school. Linda began riding the bus when she started school in 1954.

> *"School started. Linda started her first day. I went with her and stayed until 12-school out. Rested and ironed in afternoon."*
>
> —Wednesday, Sept. 1, 1954

On August 8, 1953, Carter Jr. married Donna Marie Talley. This was the first son to marry, and the house was busy on the wedding day. Carter was the only one laid back. Pat found him taking a nap just minutes before his wedding. She had been shining his shoes, and when she went in and woke him up, he chased her outside with a towel.

Carter and Donna moved into the Dr. Kingsolving house and had their first two children, Carol Ann in 1956, and Frank in 1958. In 1956 Carter Jr. went through training with State Farm Insurance in Abingdon and started the Garrett Agency in Abingdon.

1953 was the year Carter Sr. purchased a Texaco station on the Bristol Highway, and in 1958 a City Service next to it. He, Jimmy, and Gene ran the stations, which included a full-service station and mechanic garage where Carter did minor mechanical work and oil changes. Full service in the fifties meant that you would pull your car next to the pumps and someone would come out and fill up your tank, wash your windows, and check your oil. They would stand around at night and talk to the locals, and kids would come to get ice cream bars out of their ice cream machine.

A gas war occurred in the mid 1950's. The Garrett's Texaco Station sold gas for 19.9 cents a gallon. When the gas war started, Carter knew the night before that it was going up, and he warned his customers. They all ran down to get their drums filled up with as much gas as they could hold. Prices did go up the next day, and topped out at 23.9 cents a gallon.

With the gas stations and school buses keeping the family busy, the farm could still not be overlooked. It produced tobacco, hay, wheat, and oats. They also raised cows, pigs, chickens, and horses.

Mildred arose at 4:30 each morning to get the men off to the gas station and school bus runs, and then Pat and Linda to school. On Sunday mornings, rising was just as early. Mildred prepared a large Sunday lunch of meats, rolls, salads, and desserts for the whole Garrett family to come home to after church.

Other than going to the movies, the family enjoyed going to the Hilo Burger, which was the first drive through diner in the community. The Howard Johnson motel had a restaurant in town, which was the only restaurant where you could go eat a full meal.

> *"Carter, Linda, Patty and I went to Bristol Paramount to see "The Greatest Show on Earth." Oh, what a rainy night."*
>
> —Wednesday, Nov. 19, 1952

> *"Circle at Mrs. Margaret's. Patty, Linda and I went tonight. Sonny took us to see our car, Ford at Crabtree."*
>
> —Thursday, Aug. 19, 1954

> *"Ironed some. Cleaned house. Sonny and Donna here a while in P.M. Tonight Gene took us to Paramount to see "No Business Like Show Business." Real good."*
>
> —Saturday, Jan.1, 1954

Penicillin was developed to help the military with wounds and increase surgery survival rates. In 1943, the required clinical trials were performed, and penicillin was shown to be the most effective antibacterial agent to date. Penicillin was available in quantity to treat allied soldiers wounded on D-Day. As production was increased, the price dropped from nearly priceless in 1940, to twenty dollars per dose in July 1943, and fifty-five cents per dose by 1946. In 1948, Andrew J. Moyer was granted a patent for a method of the mass production of penicillin.

"Linda real sick – headache and high fever. Called Dr. Brillehart at 3:30. He came about 9:30. Said she had strep throat. Gave penicillin. Temp 103 1/2."

—Wednesday, Feb. 2, 1955

Jonas Salk made huge medical history in 1952, when he developed the first polio vaccine. Salk introduced it to the world on April 12, 1955. It consisted of an injected dose of inactivated (dead) poliovirus. Albert Sabin used attenuated poliovirus to developed an oral vaccine. Human trials of the vaccine began in 1957, and it was licensed in 1962. Soon after Salk's vaccine was licensed in 1955, children's vaccination campaigns were launched. The March of Dimes promoted a mass immunization campaign in the U.S. After the campaign, the annual number of polio cases fell from 35,000 in 1953 to 5,600 by 1957 and only 161 by 1961.

"Patty took polio shot. Made her awfully sick. Wayne Able drove her home."

—Monday, Oct. 29, 1956

"Patty not too much better."

—Tuesday, Oct. 30, 1956

"Spent today with Mama. Patty went back to school. Tonight Patty and I went with Linda to Trick-or-Treat. She had a big time."

—Wednesday, Oct. 31, 1956

In order to prevent the spread of communism in Southeast Asia, President Eisenhower sent hundreds of military advisors to aid the Republic of South Vietnam. Vietnam split in half in 1954, after fighting a war to gain independence from France. Vietnamese Communists gained control of North Vietnam under the power of Ho Chi Minh.

The 1956 election brought Dwight D. Eisenhower back into office. A Republican, Eisenhower entered the 1952 presidential race to crusade against Communism, Korea, and corruption. As President, Eisenhower concluded negotiations with China to end the Korean War. He gave priority to inexpensive nuclear weapons while reducing the funding for the other military forces to keep pressure on the Soviet Union. He started NASA to compete in the space race, removed Joseph McCarthy from power, and left a lot of power to his vice president, Richard Nixon. He enlarged the scope of Social Security and sent federal troops to enforce the Supreme Court's ruling to desegregate schools.

With so much going on in the country, and Eisenhower's heart trouble that he dealt with in his first term, many wondered if he would run a second term. He did run and won with enormous popularity.

> *"(Election Day) Carter brought a load of gas over. Ate dinner. Listened to election news tonight."*
>
> —Tuesday, Nov. 6, 1956

> *"Gene took me up home for dinner. Spent day with Mama. 'Election Argument.' Rainy and cold tonight."*
>
> —Thursday, Nov. 8, 1956.

With the Cold War still threatening America, the federal government responded to heightened public anxiety by creating the Federal Civil Defense Administration (FCDA), later called the Office of Civil Defense, to instruct the public about how to prepare for a nuclear assault. Under President Eisenhower, information was distributed to educate Americans about how they could protect themselves. Linda, at age eight, would have bomb drills in school. She also had classes that taught students how to build a bomb shelter, also known as a fallout shelter, and what to put in them.

The government felt that if the public was educated and built these fallout shelters, that another disaster like the one in Nagasaki and Hiroshima would not be as deadly if America was attacked. Some families took this seriously, and if they had plenty of money, they took heed of this warning. Others used cellars or basements as their fallout shelters. The standard drill in school was an alarm that went off and children were to duck under their desks.

Music was looked to as a way to keep minds off world events. Rock and Roll music emerged in the fifties as the popular music choice for teenagers. Patty had dances at school including her prom, where the record player would play records of Elvis Presley, Chuck Berry, Buddy Holly, and Rickie Nelson. Elvis Presley was a young boy from Memphis, Tennessee, who had a way of capturing young audiences with his good looks, fancy clothes, and swiveling hips. Patty watched the family television set with her father the night Elvis appeared on the Ed Sullivan Show in September 1956. Carter could not believe a man would do such moves in public and on TV.

The economy was booming in the fifties. Women enjoyed shopping for their hoop skirts and bandannas, button up shirts, bobby socks, and tennis shoes. The Hoola Hoop became popular when it came on the market in 1958. The Barbie doll was introduced in 1959. She was popular among young girls who dressed her up in separately purchased outfits and styled her hair to look like a model. It changed the way women looked at themselves and the way girls played with dolls.

> *"Patty, Linda and I went to Bristol to get Linda a winter coat. Pink, $15.00. Got a girdle and bra, $19.00, and gift for baby shower."*
>
> —Saturday, Nov. 10, 1956

In 1955, Gene graduated from high school and went to ETSU on a basketball scholarship. He was a star basketball player in high school. In his first semester at State, he broke his foot and had to quit the team. He decided to quit college since he could not play ball, and he went back to helping his dad at the service station.

The family purchased a new 1955 Mercury that Carter and Mildred took on their spontaneous trip to Florida in 1956. After giving a bridal shower in their home, Carter said to Mildred, "Throw some things together and let's go driving." They ended up in Tampa and drove on to Daytona. Mildred had only the dress she was wearing to wash out and put on each day.

In 1956, Patty graduated from high school along with Jimmy who had dropped out for two years to work and then returned. Patty went on to Abingdon Technical School for a year, and then to Lees-McRae College for two years. She studied to become a medical secretary but was one test from finishing when she decided she wanted to work for Carter Jr. She worked for the Garrett Agency until Carter Jr. sold out, and she then worked for the Clifton Agency.

Gene married Agnes on June 14, 1957. In 1958 they had their first child, Vickie. Gene later went to work for Raytheon in Bristol and then drove a truck for City Service Oil Company.

In 1958 Carter and Mildred celebrated their 25th Wedding Anniversary at the Moonlight Grill. The whole family gathered at the restaurant and Patty baked a cake for the occasion. That same year, Jimmy joined the Army. After boot camp at Fort Knox, he went into active duty for six months and then into active reserves for six and a half years. When he returned from the Army he met Anne McReynolds, the future Mrs. Jim Garrett, at Trayers Drive-In in Bristol.

Carter, Mildred, and Linda
in the front yard

Carter with his new
school bus in 1952

One of Gene's friends in front of the Garrett's Texaco station

Carter

Jimmy

Gene

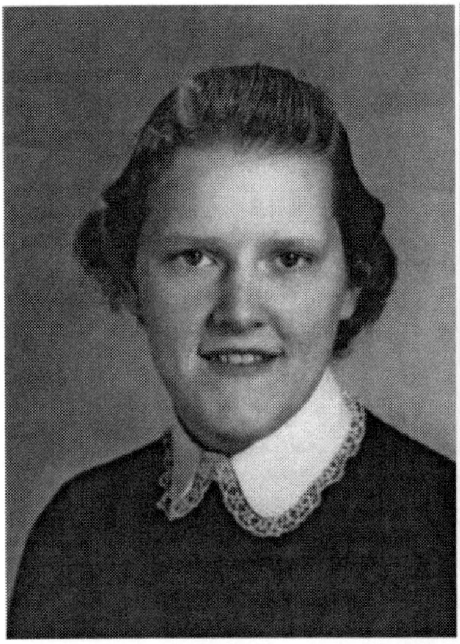

Patty

Linda

Carter and Mildred's trip to Florida in September

Mildred outside motel in Tampa

Christmas Day in Mildred's home, 1957

Chapter 6

Times Are Changing

Songs from the sixties define the generation best. Buffalo Springfield's "For What It's Worth" from 1967 was written primarily about the Vietnam War; however, it could also define other events such as the Civil Rights and Women's Rights Movements. All were very controversial, political, and important enough to draw crowds of protestors.

Although the fifties were prosperous, they were still somewhat conservative. When the sixties emerged, all that was over. Americans, especially the "Baby Boomers" from the previous generation, stood in picket lines, watched classmates go off to war, and watched man walk on the moon. All that was intertwined with new styles of music and new ways of self-expression.

Life in the country escaped some of the turmoil, but the world's events were happening in Mildred's living room through her television set. The Garrett family started going their separate ways, and each one would experience the new generation differently.

History was made in 1960, when a presidential debate was seen on television for the first time. Now, Americans could see who they were going to vote for, and it was between a very experienced Richard Nixon and the young John F. Kennedy. New times called for new blood, and Kennedy was elected as the thirty-fifth President of the United States. He gave hope and excitement to a new and changing generation.

The Soviet Union beat Americans into space with Cosmonaut Yuri Gagarin becoming the first human to orbit the earth in 1961. Alan Shepard became the first U.S. astronaut into space later that year. Man going into space was one event in history that Mildred found most unbelievable. People thought that sending something into space would hurt the atmosphere. Out of all the inventions, airplanes, new fashions and trends, hearing of a man going into space was amazing.

In 1960, a spontaneous combustion broke out in the Garrett garage. Carter Sr. and Jimmy had been painting a truck in the garage earlier in the day. After the family had gone to bed, an explosion woke them up and Carter ran out to see flames taking over his garage. Mildred, Patty, and Linda started carrying things out of the house, which was only feet from the fire. Linda carried out dresser drawers. In the panic and hurry, Mildred remembered her old white work shoes and a fern. Jimmy was just coming home from a date, and saw the flames blazing and thought the house was on fire. He rushed to help put out the flames. A miracle happened that day, when a gust of wind blew the flames in the opposite direction and the house was spared. In the end, the three-stall garage, smokehouse, wash house, wood house, and outhouse were destroyed.

In 1961, Carter Jr. sold his insurance agency and went to work for Blue Cross Blue Shield Association. In 1963, he and his family, now including two more children, Allen, born in 1960 and Greg, born in 1961, moved to Roanoke where he continued working for Blue Cross Blue Shield.

Gene and Agnes's second daughter Angela was born in 1962. Mildred now had six grandchildren who came to visit quite often. She loved being a grandmother.

On November 2, 1962, Jimmy married Anne McReynolds. After returning from the Army, he began driving a gasoline truck for Lemon Transport. He enjoyed driving a truck, but Anne didn't want him being gone and out on the highway, so in 1964 he decided to try something new. Mildred showed him a brochure they had received from Carter's cousin Clarence, who owned Garrett Freightlines in Pocatello, Idaho. His company was celebrating their 50th Anniversary.

Clarence A. Garrett had moved to Pocatello from Virginia at

the age of nineteen. He and his brother Oscar moved there to become entrepreneurs. They started a grocery store in 1910, which closed in 1913. Clarence had always dreamed of owning a transporting company, and after the store closed, he purchased his first truck with the help of Oscar, cousin Leonard, and a bank loan. The 1913 Reo truck was a one cylinder half ton, which cost $525 plus freight. They were the first to haul by truck. They started out doing local hauling and it grew from there, hauling to Utah, Montana, and to Los Angeles by 1934. The main terminal was always located in Pocatello, but they later added more terminals, eventually including a total of sixty-seven terminals and 3500 units to serve the western United States.

Clarence was called the "Dean of Western Transportation." Garrett Freightlines was the oldest motor carrier in the country, and the first to use diesel engines in their trucks and refrigerator units in trailers. They were also the first to run double and triple trailers.

When Jimmy and Anne read through the 50th Anniversary brochure, they called Clarence and asked if he would like for Jimmy to move out and work for him. Clarence was elated by the offer and told him to come right on. On June 30, 1964, the couple moved to Pocatello and on to Portland, Oregon, where Jimmy worked as a customer service employee for Garrett Freightlines. This trip was quite an adventure for the newlyweds. No one from the Green Spring Community had driven across country, and at twenty-nine years old, Jimmy didn't know what to expect. They traveled on two lane roads the whole way, and entered Pocatello on roads that were built through mountains. A sign appeared that said "No Fence Laws" and "Watch out for cattle." Cattle would run out in the middle of the roads. Jimmy had never seen anything like this before! They rented a furnished apartment in Portland, Oregon.

The 1960's were a time of fear for many. With another war on the brink for Americans, and political hands changing, another form of war began that had started well before Mildred even knew it existed. The Civil Rights Movement heightened in 1963 with the leadership of Dr. Martin Luther King, an American clergyman and activist.

Segregation existed in the United States for as long as Mildred was a child. She remembers tenants on her father's farm who were black and worked on the farm. Her family treated them no different than the whites, but it was known in the South that blacks and whites had their own places, and that was not together. She can remember one of the workers who helped during threshing season was black. When dinnertime came, he always sat at another table away from the others.

The Garrett children never grew up around many blacks unless it was working next to them on the farm. Patty remembered the first family of blacks she ever saw in Abingdon lived across the street from Aunt Maude's house. When going into town to the soda shop and lunch counter, the blacks were not allowed to eat next to the white people. They had their own section. When riding the bus in town, they had to sit in the back. None of this affected the Garretts out in the country, and Mildred always felt that the Lord didn't make distinction between blacks and whites.

By the 1960's, blacks were starting to take a stand for equal rights. In southern states, primarily Mississippi and Alabama, people started to protest, hold demonstrations and rallies. The Civil Rights Movement had begun.

On August 28, 1963, in a March on Washington D.C, over 250,000 supporters of the Civil Rights Movement gathered to promote meaningful civil rights legislation and end racial segregation. They also wanted to end the police brutality and killings that had happened throughout the South and gain equal opportunities for employment and education. It was during this march that Dr. Martin Luther King gave his famous "I Have A Dream" speech, which was widely broadcast. The Civil Rights Act of 1964 was passed the following year, which prohibited n based on race, color, religion, sex, and national deral and state governments as well as some public

ca's style of music also changed through several very famous black performers. Berry Gordy, a songwriter in Detroit, quit his job in 1957 to pursue music as a full time career after hitting the pop charts. In January 1960, he purchased a house in Detroit and called it *Hitsville U.S.A.* Motown was born. Motown played an important role in the racial integration of music in the sixties and seventies. "The Motown Sound" was a style of soul music with a distinct pop influence.

The sixties had a music revolution, not only for Motown, but all types of music popularized. The Beach Boys had started a hip, fun style of Rock and Roll with beachy tunes such as *Good Vibrations* and *I Get Around.* The Beatles gave Elvis a run for his money in 1964 when they visited the U.S. from Britain, starting what was later known as the "British Invasion." Soon the Rolling Stones, Herman's Hermits, and others came to the U.S. to spread a new British style Rock and Roll. Acid Rock and Folk music also became popular, along with Country. In 1969, Woodstock was held, which showcased Rock music to a crowd of 400,000 fans. Janis Joplin, Jimi Hendrix, and Grateful Dead were some of the performers. Not only was it a time of music, but also a time of rampant drug use, drinking, and the beginning of the "Self Expression Era."

In the sixties, Patty went with a tour group on a trip to Hawaii with a neighbor, Daphne Jones. Hawaii had become part of the United States in 1959. Carter and Mildred drove Patty to Nashville to catch the plane. Mildred had never seen a plane take off after dark, so when she saw the flames spit out under the plane, she thought it was on fire. She hurried back to the motel to listen to the radio and see if the plane had gone down.

Mildred and Carter spent the night, and the next day they enjoyed Nashville. They went to the Ryman Auditorium to see the

Grand Ole Opry for the first time. The Grand Ole Opry was a country and western music show that was broadcast live from Nashville. It had aired on WSM-AM on Mildred's radio since the thirties, and featured entertainers such as Roy Acuff, Minnie Pearl, Little Jimmie Dickens, and Patsy Cline.

The world stopped turning on November 22, 1963 when word came out that President Kennedy had been shot in his motorcade on a parade route through Dallas, Texas. His wife Jackie was sitting next to him where she witnessed the shocking event. Walter Cronkite, popular television news anchor, made the announcement that the President had been taken to the hospital. Thirty-five minutes later he announced that the President had died. The world mourned with Kennedy's wife Jacqueline and his two children, Caroline and John Jr.

Mildred was in the Sears and Roebuck store downtown Bristol with Patty when they heard the news. They were walking through the store to exit, and saw everyone gathered around the television set. Linda was still in school and was sitting in her math class at John Battle. The news was announced over the intercom. The family gathered that night to watch the news and see the Vice President Lyndon B. Johnson being sworn in on "Air Force One" flying Kennedy's body back to Washington. In the following days, the funeral was televised and Mildred remembers watching John Jr. saluting his father's coffin as it rolled by.

President Kennedy had sent more advisors to Vietnam during his three years as president. In 1964, U.S. President Lyndon B. Johnson reported that North Vietnam had attacked U.S. Navy ships along Vietnam's coast. Slowly, American troops began shipping to Vietnam, and by the end of 1965 nearly 80,000 U.S. troops were in South Vietnam. Young men from eighteen to twenty-six signed up to fight another war. Several of Linda's classmates signed up after graduation and one boy from her class went off to war and never returned.

Gene left the City Service Oil Company and went to the

police academy for twenty-one weeks in Richmond. On July 1, 1964 he became a Virginia State Trooper. In 1968 he was awarded with the DSA award from the Chilhowie Jaycee's. He had served with them as president for two years and internal vice president for one year. As Jaycee State Vice President in 1968, he was one of two troopers to be selected to appear in the 1970 edition of *Outstanding Young Men in America.*

On July 1, 1965, Patty, Linda, Mildred, and Carter took their first trip cross-country to Portland, Oregon, to see Jimmy and Anne. They went in Carter Jr.'s brand new Buick. He had purchased the luxury car with air conditioning, which had just started being installed in cars. He didn't want the family going through the Mojave Desert in the extreme heat without air, so he insisted they borrow his car.

The trip lasted over a week and covered more than 6,000 miles. They saw several sights and scenery that they had never seen, including the Painted Desert, Yellowstone National Park, Redwood Forest, and the Golden Gate Bridge. Jimmy and Anne moving West provided the family an opportunity to see parts of the country they might have never seen otherwise. They enjoyed visiting with Jimmy and Anne and Clarence Garrett. They toured the Garrett Freightlines Headquarters and Clarence's ranch.

The brand new Buick really got broke-in during their trip. An air hose busted in Kansas, the windshield cracked, and the trunk was accidentally locked up with everyone's luggage in it. It made the trip very memorable. Mildred woke up at 4:30 each morning to make instant coffee in plastic cups before they hit the road. When traveling, she liked to get an early start.

Linda graduated from high school in 1966, a month before Patty married John Testerman. She met John at Statzers Drive-In in Abingdon. Three days after they married, they moved to Graham, North Carolina, where she got a job working for Burlington Industries Pioneer Plant as the plant manager's secretary.

Linda went to Carson Newman College in the fall and majored in Sociology. The whole family was physically separated, but all talked on the phone and wrote letters. They enjoyed the summers when they all came together at the Garrett house with Carter and Mildred. Linda and Patty came in whenever their schedules allowed. Mildred missed her children very much, but knew that they had to do what made them happy and she knew she didn't want to hold any of them back.

Carter continued working on the farm and doing carpentry work. He helped to build several houses in the community, and built cabinets and furniture. Mildred continued taking care of her mother who had been bedridden for the past twenty-one years and suffered with seizures. Mildred did the laundry for her parents, cleaned house, and took meals to them. Her mother died in 1969. In a way, it was a blessing to see her suffering end, but Mildred's mother had played such a huge role in her life. Her mother was so young when Mildred was born, that she felt as though she had grown up with her. Her father missed his wife, "Love." They had spent a lifetime of honeymoon bliss together. Mildred saw them pick at each other and flirt years after she was grown.

The sixties was also a time of great sports popularity. Baseball was already popular, but football and boxing became very popular as well. In 1967, the first AFL-NFL Championship Game was held. Super Bowl I was aired on January 15, in Los Angeles, California. The Greenbay Packers won over the Kansas City Chiefs.

African Americans played a huge role in sports. Jackie Robinson became the first to be inducted into the Baseball Hall of Fame in 1962. In 1964, boxer Cassius Clay "Mohammed Ali" beat Sonny Liston in seven rounds to win heavyweight championship.

Families enjoyed sitting around the television sipping on Coca Cola, now purchased in cans, and watching shows such as *The Flintstones, My Three Sons,* and *The Andy Griffith Show. Bonanza* and *Gunsmoke* were two of Carter's favorite westerns that he and Linda enjoyed watching together. Mildred's favorite show that she would continue to watch throughout her life was *Days of our Lives*, which became a popular soap opera in 1965, and aired as thirty minute daily programs. As soap operas grew in popularity in the seventies, they would extend to one hour.

A lot of time was spent traveling in the sixties for Mildred and Carter. Carter fixed up a Ford truck with a covered bed that he transformed into a camper. He built a cabinet and put two beds in it. They would pack up a little portable gas stove and supplies and take off on trips, mostly to see their children. They took several trips to the Smoky Mountains and area campgrounds.

In 1968 they took their second trip to Portland to see Jimmy, Anne and their new grandson Stephen, who was born in June. Mildred kept her diary while on the trip and documented where they spent each night. After a nice trip to see Jimmy's family, they headed back home, stopping to visit friends and family along the way. Mildred enjoyed the trips in the camper with Carter, and would wake up and fix breakfast each morning on their stove.

> *"Left Beaverton, Oregon at 8:30 a.m. Oh how sad to part."*
>
> —October 24, 1968

> *"Drove to Boise and spent the night at Traveler's Motel. Same one as we had when we went out."*
>
> —October 25

> *"Drove to Pocatello and spent afternoon and night with Dorothy. She took us out to supper."*
>
> —October 26

> *"Left Dorothy at 11 a.m. Drove to Rock Springs, Wyo. Spent night at Albert's Traveler's Court."*
>
> —October 27

"Drove to Kimball, Neb. Spent night at Seward, Neb. at Dakota Camp."

—October 28

"Spent night at Mt. Pleasant, Iowa."

—October 29

"Drove into Stevens' at 10:30 a.m. Visited them about 3 hours. Drove on to Crawfordsville (motel) Indiana."

—October 30

"Spent tonight at Corbin, Ky. in camping park back of Gulf Service Station."

—October 31

"Arrived at Carson Newman College at 2 p.m. Spent 3 hours with Linda. Drove home. Got here at 8:30. A perfect trip. How we enjoyed it."

—November 1

In the summer of 1969, on a visit to North Carolina to see Patty, and to pick up Linda from her summer job and take her back to Carson Newman, Carter had a heart attack. The afternoon they arrived, Patty took them to Sears in the mall, and it was there that Carter started having chest pains. They took him on to the hospital where the doctors informed them that he was having a heart attack. It was severe, and in the sixties, they did not have advanced medical treatments. He spent time in the hospital and at Patty's house recovering. He and Mildred went on to Roanoke to visit Carter Jr. afterward, and then on home, where Carter had to slow down. The prescription for a heart attack was not surgery or pills, but rest.

On July 21, 1969, Americans tuned in to watch Neil Armstrong step on the surface of the moon. Through the power of live television, his famous words were heard across the country. "That's one small step for man… one giant leap for mankind." This event brought excitement to some and fear to others. If we had enough technology to do something like land a man on the moon, what were other countries capable of doing to us? The Apollo 11 crew made history, and they were greeted home with parades and celebrations.

In 1969, the war in Vietnam was still raging and many thought this to be a needless war. This war was the first to be brought home through live television. On the evening news you saw the American troops in the jungles with their guns and desperate and worn looks on their faces.

On December 1, 1969, the first draft lottery was held since 1942. This was a drawing using a large glass container, which held 366 blue plastic balls containing birth dates from January 1, 1944 to December 31, 1950. Men born on these dates, ages eighteen to twenty-six years old, were required to report to register for the military. 1969 was the height of the Vietnam War, and the U.S. had approximately 543,000 troops in Vietnam.

Carter, Jimmy, and Mildred at Garrett Freightlines
Carter and Mildred visiting Jimmy and Anne in Portland, Oregon in 1965

Mildred's parents celebrating their birthdays in 1962

Mildred and Carter in the sixties

Traveling in the sixties

Traveling in the sixties

Chapter 7

An Empty Nest

It seems repetitive to say that the seventies were a time of change. All decades from 1911 until now brought their own set of changes, atmosphere, and new ways of thinking. The seventies for the Garrett family would also be a time of great change and sadness.

Fashions changed and "fads" were really popular for young people. Men and women were styling bell-bottoms, platformshoes, afros, and long hair. This was the decade of propaganda. People were hanging smiley face and peace sign bumper stickers on their Volkswagens, all either symbolizing peace, an end to the Vietnam war, or just happiness.

Mildred and Carter enjoyed the visits they had from their children and grandchildren who were now going into their teenage years. They would come spend weekends with their grandparents and ride horses and enjoy the country. They would have picnics and would enjoy when Patty and John would bring their boat to the lake. With Carter's health deteriorating with severe arthritis and heart trouble, he tried to take it easy and not work as hard as he had in years past.

Mildred had always dreamed of owning a hotel. She loved staying in hotels and thought it would be a fun adventure for her and Carter in their golden years. They took a motel management course out of Biscayne Bay, Florida. They finished the course, but Carter's health kept them from going into the business.

In February 1970, he had his second heart attack, and it was a major one. Doctors said his heart had split, causing extensive damage. He was in the hospital for twenty-eight days. The family was called in, thinking that he was going to die. Out of the blue one day, several were sitting in the waiting room and heard a man talking and said, "Could that be Carter Garrett?" It was. He had survived the attack, but would still have a long way to recovery. He was brought home where Mildred cared for him in a hospital bed. For months afterwards, he was in a wheel chair and on crutches. He did get well enough to see a wish come true: Linda graduating from Carson Newman in 1970. She moved to Richmond where she got a job with the YWCA as the adult activities director.

Mildred decided she needed to learn how to drive and get her driver's license after Carter had his second heart attack. She had driven cars to her parents' house and across the street to a neighbor or relatives house, but she was ready to become more independent and self-reliant. Gene taught her the basics. She studied the book for the test in the hospital while she sat with Carter. She passed her test and got her license. She was then able to drive Carter to his appointments.

Carter could not do much carpentry or farming after his heart attack, and moved his woodworking shop to their back porch. He made cookbook holders, wooden scrapbooks, pincushions, and candlesticks to pass the time away. Little did they know the progress that was being made in heart surgery.

People became more earth conscious in the seventies, and began to recycle. April 22, 1970, marked the first Earth Day, which launched the environmental movement.

Mood rings, lava lamps, and pet rocks were popular for all ages in the seventies. People were trying to find themselves in what seemed to be a time when the world was in turmoil. War was still raging at the first half of the decade. Vietnam seemed to get closer home as more soldiers were being lost in battle.

On April 30, 1970, the U.S. and South Vietnamese invaded Cambodia. This was a turning point as many turned against the war and President Nixon. People saw this as another conflict with another country, and students and campuses across the nation were protesting. Rivalries broke out between police officers and students, leading to many deaths. On April 24, 1970, an anti-war march occurred in Washington, which was one of the largest gatherings since the march against segregation.

> *"Washed-Sowed watermelon, cantaloupe and cucumbers this AM. Washed living room curtains. Late- went up and set out 25 tomato and pepper plants. Tired tonight."*
>
> —June 7, 1971

> *"Went to Abingdon to Bank and get medicine then to Bristol. We ate lunch at McDonalds. I ordered me some shoes at Burrouphs $18.25. Got rugs for front porch, etc. Nice day."*
>
> —June 9, 1971

A life-changing event happened on May 24, 1972. Carter and Mildred were out plowing the garden together when Carter collapsed next to her. She tried to give him "Artificial Resuscitation" as it was called then, but it was too late. The ambulance came and took him away and he was later pronounced dead at the age of sixty-two. Mildred had lost her husband with whom she had spent the last thirty-nine years. The day Mildred was at the funeral home making arrangements, her father was taken to the hospital. Carter died on Wednesday and was buried on Saturday. Her dad died the day Carter was buried, and they had his funeral on Monday. He was eighty-seven years old.

It was an extremely hard time for Mildred. Her father had not even been sick. He started feeling poorly on Friday and was taken to the hospital where he died Saturday. Mildred visited him before going to Carter's funeral. She was living in a state of shock, but she remained strong with the help of God and her family.

The kids took time about staying with Mildred until all the activity was over. It hit her the hardest when she spent that first night alone. Linda decided to move home in 1973, and she got a job with the YWCA in Bristol as the youth and adult program director. Before taking that job, she and Mildred drove to Portland, Oregon, to visit Jimmy and Anne. When they got out there, Linda was going to stay and work for a year; however, she did not find a job, so she returned home with Mildred. Mildred thought she was going to fly back home if Linda stayed, and she was nervous about getting on an airplane for the first time. Jimmy took her to the airport to show her around and go through the steps, but she ended up not having to fly.

When they returned home, they found out that their little dog Tippi that Gene had kept for them got loose and ran into the road. It was killed. Tippi was like another member of the family and was Carter's pal. He enjoyed it around the house and would let it sit on his lap and watch TV with him. Now with Tippi and Carter both gone, the house was very lonely.

A huge court case took place in 1973, which would be known as Roe vs. Wade. After the hearings, the Supreme Court decision deemed abortion a fundamental right under the United States Constitution, thereby subjecting all laws attempting to restrict it to the standard of strict scrutiny. Free expression, drug use, and the recession, in which the economy was in the worst shape in forty years, all led to couples conceiving out of wedlock. These tough times for young couples led many to think more about abortion, which the Christian world did not agree with. This led to more protests for either pro-life or pro-choice.

1973 brought an oil crisis to Americans who waited in line at gas stations only to find out that there was no gas. The government controlled the prices, limiting the price of old oil and allowing newly discovered oil to be sold for more. The rule was intended to promote oil exploration, but ended in rationing which led to long lines at the gas pumps, violence, and truck drivers going on strike.

On August 9, 1974, President Richard Nixon resigned. He was facing an impeachment after he was found being involved in the Watergate scandal that had occupied the political scene since

June 1972. Five men were arrested after being caught breaking into the Democratic National Committee headquarters at the Watergate complex. The payments the burglars were receiving were connected to a slush fund used by the committee to re-elect Nixon. Nixon and his staff members were involved and faced impeachment. After he resigned on national television, Gerald Ford succeeded him and issued a pardon to Nixon.

The Vietnam War slowed down in the seventies. On April 30, 1975, at 8:35 a.m., the last Americans departed from Saigon, concluding the U.S. presence in Vietnam. North Vietnamese troops poured into Vietnam, leading to the South's surrender. The war was over! Vietnam had become one country but under communist rule.

In 1975, Linda became the youngest executive director of the YWCA in Bristol. This was a huge step for Linda, and made Mildred very proud to watch her daughter on television announcing activities and information about the YWCA. In 1978 Linda was awarded "Woman of the Year" by the Zeta Gamma Chapter of the Beta Sigma Phi Sorority. It was an award given to women who displayed outstanding qualities of leadership and community service.

Linda left the YWCA later that year and became a field consultant with the American Heart Association. Although the YWCA was a woman's organization and its directors were women, it was still a big deal for women to hold titles in the workforce. In the seventies, women's rights were being fought just as much as the war on racism. On March 22, 1972, The Equal Rights Amendment was passed by Congress and sent to the states for ratification. The amendment reads: "Equality of rights under the law shall not be denied or abridged by the United States or by any State on account of sex." It was never ratified by enough states to become part of the Constitution.

In the late seventies, a new type of music led to a new type of dance craze known as "Disco Fever." Nightclubs and dance halls turned into disco clubs. With a disco ball hanging from the ceiling and psychedelic lights flooding the room, people put on their platform shoes and danced the night away. Linda was with the YWCA at the time, where disco classes were taught and she participated in some.

In 1979, Sony introduced the Walkman, which was a cassette tape player small enough to attach to your hip with headphones. Cassette tapes replaced eight-track tapes from the seventies, although records were still in existence that played on record players. Phonograph records were replaced with LPN's and 45's, which became a thin and lighter record made of vinyl. These sold through the seventies and into the eighties.

Mildred's favorite president was Jimmy Carter. She liked his qualities of humility and truthfulness. Carter became president in 1977. He was a democrat from Georgia. He was also a peanut farmer and naval officer. While in office he created the Department of Energy and Department of Education. He emphasized human rights. The end of his term marked several big events of the decade, including the 1979 energy crisis, the Soviet invasion of Afghanistan, and the 1980 eruption of Mount St. Helens located in Washington state.

On August 16, 1977, Elvis Presley died of a heart attack in his home in Memphis. He was only forty-two years old. President Jimmy Carter released a statement that Elvis had "permanently changed the face of American popular culture." Around 80,000 people lined the processional route of the funeral in Memphis. Both Linda and Patty were Elvis fans and Linda had attended one of his concerts at Freedom Hall in Johnson City.

Jimmy was working for Garrett Freightlines when it was bought out by ANR in 1979. He moved to Salt Lake City, Utah, in April 1979, and became division manager and later regional vice president. Patty had been the plant manager's secretary at Burlington Industries for ten years, but in 1976 was transferred to the division office as an executive assistant. Mildred was once again so proud of her children and all their accomplishments.

Mildred stayed busy working around the house and spending time with her children and grandchildren. She enjoyed Linda being close and bringing friends over to the house for parties and picnics. Linda would bring the YWCA Young Adult Group to the house, where she and Mildred would cook for them and they would play croquet and badminton.

By 1978, Mildred decided she was ready to find a job that would get her out of the house and bring in some extra money. She had never worked outside the home and didn't really know what she wanted to do. She had dreams of things she wanted to do with her life, but they always came back to family and children. She had always enjoyed teaching the young people at church and did babysitting at the YWCA.

Linda showed Mildred a want ad in the paper. A couple needed a babysitter for their four-month-old baby girl. Mildred called and was interviewed and got the job! Lindsey was a blessing for her. Mildred got up early in the morning and drove to the Cold Spring Community where she kept Lindsey during the day. As Lindsey grew, they would play games and have tea parties. It was a joy to have something to do and someone else to look after. She missed her house being full. Lindsey and her parents, Renny and Linda King, became a second family to her.

(Last family photo taken before Carter's death)
Family get-together at Patty's house in 1971

Carter Jr's Family:
Allen's girlfriend, Allen, Carter Jr., Donna, Carol Ann, Greg, Frank, and Kathy

Jimmy's Family

Hall Family: Charles, Lowry, Ricky, Karen, Barbara, Sandra, Harold, and Oma

Chapter 8

Moving On

By 1980, Mildred had lived by herself for several years and was adjusting. She had great friends and family who lived around her. She now had seven grandchildren and three great-grandchildren who would visit often. She still did church work and attended circle meetings. Her brother Dee was diagnosed with kidney disease and she would help his wife Dorothy take him for dialysis treatments. He died in 1980. She also kept Lindsey who was getting ready to start school in a couple years.

The 1980's could be summed up in two famous sayings of the time; "If you have it, flaunt it," and "Shop til you drop." The economy had once again become that of a consumer society and young people looked up to the rich and famous as their role models. The media kept up with the rise and fall of the rich. The average salary was $15,757. People started charging things and credit cards were used more for everyday objects rather than only large purchases. The money and fame craze was fueled by a romantic fairytale event in 1981. In July, Prince Charles married Diana Spencer at St. Paul's Cathedral in London. 750 million people watched on their TV's, and 600,000 lined the streets of London.

Technology was the best it had ever been. The invention of boom boxes, video games, and now the personal computer were all the rage. An American family shown on a television show would be wearing their designer clothes, cruising to the beach in their minivan with the kids in the back seat playing their boom box or listening to their Walkman. Girls wore headbands with hot pink hair and long earrings. Boys wore their sunglasses with high top shoes and spiked hair.

Mildred jumped into the fads of the eighties when she

purchased a pair of purple Nike tennis shoes. Fads were flamboyant and colorful for adults. Anything big was bold, from hairstyles to shoulder pads. She received a Cabbage Patch Doll for Christmas one year. The new toy was one of many that emerged from the eighties. From Strawberry Shortcake to Teenage Mutant Ninja Turtles, popular toys in the eighties were first a cartoons and then toys.

One of televisions most loved and viewed news anchors retired in 1980. Walter Cronkite was the voice America heard when man walked on the moon and when Kennedy was assassinated. His CBS position was replaced by Dan Rather. Talk shows such as the Phil Donahue Show and the Oprah Winfrey Show were becoming popular. Most of these shows put everyday people on the spot to discuss issues going on in the world such as rape, drug abuse, and divorce.

In 1981, Ronald Reagan, a former radio, film and television actor, and former governor of California, became the 40th President of the United States. Only sixty-nine days into his presidency, an assassination attempt was made. He and three others were struck by gunfire outside the Washington Hilton Hotel. He fought for his life through surgery and recovered.

AIDS was first reported on June 5, 1981. A strand was reported in a group of homosexual men in Los Angeles. After determining that the disease was not isolated to the homosexual community, the disease was given the name AIDS, Acquired Immune Deficiency Syndrome. The disease slowly shuts down the immune systems and allows opportunistic disease and tumors to enter. The awareness of this disease and the homosexual community led to a huge gay rights movement in the eighties.

In 1980, Linda met her husband Parvon, a friend of Gene's neighbor. After meeting him at Gene's house and Parvon being very persistent, he proposed months later and she said yes. On April 4, 1981, they were married at Cleveland Presbyterian Church. Parvon worked at L.C. King Manufacturing Company in

Bristol, and Linda moved into his house that he had built in Bristol. Linda got pregnant in December 1982.

Mildred was at Linda's house getting ready to enjoy her birthday dinner on September 30, 1983, when Linda went into labor. Parvon drove her to the hospital while Mildred ate her dinner by herself. The next day, she got a call that her last grandchild, Patricia "Renee" was born.

Gene injured his back while at work and had to retire early in 1981 as a state trooper. By this time, he and his wife Agnes had two grandchildren and had moved their residence over ten times. By 1986, they had moved seventeen times in twenty years, buying and reselling in a real-estate friendly economy. Their last move was to Crossville, Tennessee, where they both enjoyed playing golf.

During 1982, the nation endured a deep recession. Business bankruptcies rose fifty percent over the previous year. In 1983, the economy rebounded and sustained a period of economic growth.

During the eighties, Carter Jr. left his job with Blue Cross. His son Allen had been in a serious diving accident and was paralyzed. Allen spent months in a Florida hospital where Mildred made a trip to visit him. Jimmy had gone from regional vice president of ANR Freight to being unemployed, and Patty had gone through a divorce. It was in rough times, however, that Mildred looked for happiness and found strength. She passed that characteristic on to her children. They rose above the difficult times, and in the long run would become extremely successful and provide their mother with all her desires throughout her golden years.

In 1984, Carter Jr. started his own independent insurance brokerage and consultant firm, Employee Benefits Management, in Roanoke. Later, he had another branch in Abingdon and Staunton, Virginia. After ANR downsized and Jimmy lost his position, he started RT Systems in Salt Lake City in 1990. He took the business from no trucks or drivers to sixty-eight trucks, bringing in $1 million a month. Patty remained in her home in

Graham, North Carolina. She enjoyed her dog Tina, and all the friends she had made in Graham. She continued to work at Burlington Industries.

The hard times came to Mildred in the eighties-- not financially, but physically. Her diary entry from January 25, 1985:

> *"Oh what a day! Went to get mail and fell on ice. Took almost an hour to get back to the house, but the Lord helped me drag my broken hip in. Took 2 hours to get to the phone to call Linda. I was suffering. So sick. Claudia came and packed my things. Called Life Savings Crew. Then Linda and Parvon came. Lee came to help. We got to the hospital on icy roads. Took x-rays. Had broken hip. So sick. Was admitted to ICU so they could monitor my heart."*

The next day, Mildred had surgery on her hip and then stayed in the hospital until February 6, when she went to Linda's to stay and recover. She enjoyed the snowy days at Linda and Parvon's, and enjoyed playing with Renee. She went to stay with Patty in North Carolina on March 24, and stayed there for over a month. It was difficult to go back to her own house after three months. It was then that she started getting scared to live alone. She had two break-ins at her house, both while she was gone to town. Both stole some of her possessions.

Patty's ex-husband had given her a gun to keep by her bed and they had installed a burglar alarm in her house after the break-ins. It gave her peace of mind, but she still had moments of nervousness. One night in particular scared her, and she would remember it the rest of her days. It was in the middle of the night, and Mildred heard something outside. Startled, she arose and peeped through the window. She saw lights at a neighbor's house and something bright and red. She thought their house was on fire. She ran to the front door and pulled it open. The alarm went off and her phone started ringing asking if she was ok. "Pure stupidity" is what she told everyone. It turns out that the neighbor was unloading a new red Porsche, and the glare from the lights made it look like fire. Mildred learned not to be so quick to act; however, she stayed nervous by herself.

She decided to sell her house and move. The house that her husband had built for their growing family had served as a home where they made memories with family and friends, and where they saw good times and bad shape their memories. After looking for houses in Bristol, Mildred was led to a house in Maple Hills by one of Parvon's friends. She fell in love with the house and spent several months cleaning out and selling her old house. They laid new carpet and painted the walls at the new house and she purchased new furniture.

> *"My last day at home. I left about 1 p.m. loaded with things I had packed. T'was really sad. Came up to see my new living room suit and bedroom suit. They delivered it this AM."*
>
> —October 31, 1985.

> *"'My Moving Day." Linda left at 8 a.m. to go up home to help move as the van was to be there at 8:30. Sonny and Frankie came from Roanoke. What would I do without my children? Gene and Agnes came to Linda's about 3:30. Frankie came after me to go up and see how things looked, so Gene, Agnes, Renee and I went up. Looked so good."*
>
> —November 1, 1985.

The younger generation was facing a time when family values had gone by the wayside and teens and young adults were into drinking, drugs, and parties. By 1986, it was estimated that 20 million people were using marijuana monthly, 5 million were using cocaine, and 500,000 were using heroin. Federal workers were subject to drug testing for the first time.

A big news event that was heard on TV in the eighties was the space shuttle Challenger explosion of 1986, which killed all on board including a school teacher.

In a speech at the Brandenburg Gate, commemorating the 750th Anniversary of Berlin on June 12, 1987, President Ronald Reagan challenged Mikhail Gorbachev, General Secretary of the Communist Party of the Soviet Union, to tear down the Berlin Wall as a symbol of increasing freedom in the Eastern Bloc. In 1989, the wall was torn down, but not all at once. People chiseled away at the wall to keep pieces as souvenirs.

One of the most incredible inventions of the 20th Century was the computer. It had gone from a room-sized piece of equipment to a desktop wonder by the end of the eighties. Many thought computers had just been invented. Little did they know that they had been an idea since 1939, when Hewlett Packard was founded in California. Their HP200A Audio Oscillator was popular with engineers. Walt Disney used it for sound effects generators for the 1940's movie "Fantasia."

Americans did not know much about the use of personal computers until 1977, when the Apple II became an instant success. It had a switching power supply, keyboard, case assembly, game paddles, AC power cord, and cassette tape with computer games. When hooked into a color TV, it had great graphics. Radio Shack came out with their version called the Tandy in that same year. It was sold for $599.95. It came with manuals, so people with no knowledge of computers could operate it.

In 1984, Apple Inc. launched Macintosh, the first successful mouse-driven computer with a graphic user interface. It was seen on a commercial for the first time during the 1984 Super Bowl and sold for $2,500. Video games on the computer became popular along with the famous gaming system sold in U.S. in 1985, called the Nintendo Entertainment System (NES). The system included R.O.B. (Robotic Operating Buddy) and the games Duck Hunt and Super Mario Bros.

Children's entertainment had changed forever, and instead of playing with a stick horse and paper dolls, Mildred saw her grandchildren and great-grandchildren grow up in a world of noise, technology, and graphics.

In 1988, George H.W. Bush was elected President, and he would be the one to lead America into another war.

Mildred in front of her new home in Bristol

Linda's wedding in 1981

Gene's Family:
Rick, Angela, Agnes, Gene, Vickie, and Richard

Welcoming home granddaughter Renee, born October 1, 1983

Patty with Ladybug

Mildred with Family and Friends
Mildred with sister-in-law Dorothy and cousins Charles,
Wennie Combs, R.K., and Nancy

Best friends Ada, Nancy, Edna, Vivian, Oma, Elizabeth, Janie, Mildred, and Dorothy

Mildred with grandchildren and great-grandchildren

Celebrating December birthdays with one of Mildred's coconut cakes (Carter Jr., Donna, Mildred, and Patty)

Mildred and Renee having fun on Halloween

Grandchildren:
Stephen, Renee, Carol Ann, Frank, Allen, Angela, and Vickie
(Not pictured- Greg)

Chapter 9

"My Children Are My Fortune"

The nineties was the decade of health care, gun control, and social security reform. Violence and sex scandals dominated the media, and hundreds died in our country due to shootings and bombings. Advances in technology provided households with new forms of communication and medical advances that changed lives.

Throughout the eighties, Iraq had been an ally of the U.S.. The U.S. was concerned with Iraq's position on Israeli- Palestinian politics. The U.S. also disliked Iraqi support for many Arab and Palestinian militant groups. On August 2, 1990, Iraqi troops invaded Kuwait. The Pentagon had plans in place to aid the Saudis, and U.S. forces went on standby for their request. Secretary of Defense Dick Cheney and General Norman Schwarzkopf met with King Fahd of Saudi Arabia to brief him on the plans, which he approved. Within minutes of the meeting, orders were issued, and the largest buildup of American forces since the Vietnam War began. In the beginning it was called "Operation Desert Shield," to signify that the military was protecting the Saudis. After air war started it would be called "Operation Desert Storm," also commonly referred to as the Gulf War.

Saddam Hussein, the Iraqi leader, would become a regular household name to Americans. On February 27, 1991, President Bush declared the liberation of Kuwait. By the war's end, U.S. forces released 71,204 Iraqi prisoners to Saudi control.

Mildred's family escaped having to go into the military, and the draft that had been in existence decades earlier was no longer taking young men away from home.

Jimmy went from RT Systems in 1990 to several other companies that he owned or managed, including a consultant job, which forced him to travel a lot. Being a family man, he knew he wanted to stay home with Anne, and he resigned on a Sunday and started his own business, Peak Transport, with three other men on Wednesday. Carter continued his insurance business and Patty was still in Burlington.

Linda stayed home with Renee for the first few years and then started doing part-time secretarial work at the International Ladies Garment Workers Union headquarters in Bristol. Mildred enjoyed babysitting Renee a few days a week.

She enjoyed living in Bristol and had made many friends through a neighborhood Garden Club. She continued to drive to Cleveland Presbyterian Church every Sunday with her friend Edna, until she started attending Linda's church, Windsor Avenue Presbyterian Church in Bristol. She enjoyed going back to Cleveland from time to time. She never moved her membership, as she always felt attached to her and Carter's home church. She had been treasurer of Women of the Church for thirty-eight years before she had moved to Bristol, and had taught Sunday school and participated in circle meetings and events.

She talked the nineties away on the telephone. She now had a "cordless" phone, which she was not used to having. It was a huge change from the phone she used when she was a child.

> *"So very cold this AM. Nell called early. I called Oma to see how she was doing. She was ok. Edna called this AM. I didn't do much but talk on the phone."*
>
> —January 16, 1992.

In 1991, Mildred celebrated her 80th birthday. Family and friends gathered at Steele's Creek Park in Bristol, where they fellowshipped and reminisced.

Holidays and family reunions were very special occasions. Mildred's grandchildren now had children of their own, and when the whole Garrett family got together, she enjoyed the company of five children, eight grandchildren, and eleven great-grandchildren.

Jimmy and Anne usually came in for a visit in the summer and would spend a couple of weeks. Sometimes cousins, nieces, and nephews would attend and make the gatherings even larger.

Each of Mildred's children had their own families with children and grandchildren to share holidays with, so Christmas festivities changed in the early eighties and nineties. Mildred did keep the tradition of making an applesauce cake for each of her five children to give them and their families for Christmas.

Mildred and Patty went to Linda, Parvon, and Renee's house every Christmas Eve and enjoyed a lasagna dinner and staying up late to watch movies or talk. On Christmas morning, Renee would wake up and open her gifts from Santa. Mildred always spent most of the morning opening gifts. She had gifts from all her children and grandchildren. She always held her health and the health of others as the greatest gift of all. In the late nineties, Linda's family and Mildred spent Christmas in Patty's home twice, and in Mildred's home twice.

> *"Beautiful snowy Christmas Day. Renee got up early, 7 a.m. We had breakfast then opened our lovely gifts. The biggest gift was that everyone was well. Got so many nice things. Gene called from Vickie's. Sonny called from Myrtle Beach. Jimmy from Salt Lake. What precious ones. Had Christmas dinner about 6 p.m. Turkey, dressing, creamed potatoes, salad. Ate too much and all kinds of sweets. Went to bed late."*
>
> —December 25, 1995.

The nineties brought another decade of travel to Mildred. By the end of the nineties, Mildred had been in almost every state in the country. She took another trip to Salt Lake City to visit Jimmy and Anne. She, Patty, and Patty's friend John, went cross-country in Mildred's Chevrolet Celebrity in 1993. Mildred also went to

Florida and Disney World with Linda, Parvon, and Renee in the early nineties. She went to the beach almost every year, and enjoyed Carter Jr.'s beach house at Myrtle Beach. She went on many trips with Carter and Donna in their motor home. They took her on her first trip to Niagara Falls and Key West, Florida. She took her second trip to Niagara Falls with Jimmy, Anne, and Anne's mother Mrs. McReynolds after seeing her grandson Stephen at Cornell University in Ithaca, New York.

She went on most family vacations with Linda including a Gettysburg trip in which Renee traced the steps that Mildred's grandfather took during the Civil War. They visited several battlefields including Appomattox, where her grandfather wrapped the flag under his coat and brought it home after the surrender.

They visited the Richmond Confederate Museum where she saw that flag. It was the same flag that hung in the parlor in her home place, and was now being viewed by thousands in a museum.

She had practically seen Pigeon Forge, Tennessee built from the ground up. She remembered going there with Carter, Linda, and Patty when it was a small pit stop before going to Cherokee, North Carolina. It had now become a travel destination full of restaurants, hotels, and activities. One activity was Dollywood, where Mildred enjoyed the shows and food on several occasions.

When not traveling or visiting with family, Mildred was enjoying going to activities with Linda and Renee. Linda was a Girl Scout leader and worked in PTA. Mildred went to programs the Girl Scouts had, and became a grandmother to all of Renee's fellow troop members. She also attended school programs, ballgames, and band concerts.

Many historical events happened in the nineties. Out of all the years she listened to her family talk about politics, Mildred had never voted. In the 1992 election, she finally voted. Linda took her to Blountville and she placed her vote for Bill Clinton. Clinton won the 1992 election against George H.W. Bush and Ross Perot.

He was inaugurated at the age of forty-six, becoming the third youngest president. He took office at the end of the Cold War, and was the first president of the baby boomer generation.

In 1993, a truck bomb detonated below the north tower of the World Trade Center in New York City. It was intended to collapse both towers, but in the end killed seven people and injured thousands. Later in April 1995, a federal building in Oklahoma City, Oklahoma was bombed, killing 168 men, women, and children. Suspect Timothy McVeigh claimed he bombed in retaliation for the 1993 Waco Massacre. The 1996 Summer Olympics were held in Atlanta, Georgia. During the festivities in Centennial Olympic Park, a bomb was set off, killing two and injuring 111. All these bombings lead to awareness of domestic and international terrorism as a potential threat to the U.S. It was one of the first times since the nuclear war scare of the fifties that Americans feared war on their home front.

In 1992, the World Wide Web was created, and for the first time, people could turn on their computers to get the daily news and headlines as they happened. This changed the way Americans viewed communication and media. People were emailing and chatting "online." In 1989, fifteen percent of Americans had a computer in their homes, and by the end of the nineties, up to fifty percent had them. Cell phones were also an invention Mildred never had and could not understand. They went from a bulky piece of equipment in a bag to a hand size flip phone. People were walking through stores and driving talking on their phones. It was definitely the electronic age!

In 1995, "The Trial of the Century" was aired on almost every local channel on cable TV, and Mildred was front and center to see if O.J. Simpson would be found guilty. O.J. Simpson was a former football star and actor who was tried on two counts of murder following the death of his ex-wife Nicole Brown Simpson and her friend Ronald Goldman. After a very long low speed chase that captured the media's attention, to the nine-month trial in California,

Americans literally put their lives on hold to watch the "not guilty" verdict be given on October 3. The verdict cost an estimated $480 million dollar loss in productivity across the U.S., as people postponed meetings, delayed using the bathroom, and long distance telephone calls stopped. President Clinton was briefed on security measures, preparing for rioting that might break out over the verdict. It was by far the most publicized trial in history.

In August 1997, Diana Princess of Whales, died in a car crash in Paris, France. It was not only devastating for her country, but also for the United States. The whole world had put her in the same category as Mother Teresa, who ironically died only a month later, in September 1997. Both women were known for their charity work done all over the world. The world also mourned for the family of Princess Diana. She left behind her two sons, William and Harry, to be raised by their father, Prince Charles.

The movie of the decade sent Mildred to the movie theater for the first time in over twenty years. *Titanic* was released in December 1997, and achieved acclaim that gave it fourteen Academy Award nominations and eleven Oscar wins, receiving Best Picture and Best Director. It was the first film to hit the billion-dollar mark, with a worldwide gross of over $1.8 billion. James Cameron took the idea from his fascination with shipwrecks. In 1985, the *Titanic* ship was discovered. The ship that went down the year after Mildred was born was now becoming one of the most famous disasters of all time. The movie, starring Leonardo DiCaprio and Kate Winslet, was amazing for Mildred to see on the big screen, and after hearing about the actual disaster as a young child, she watched history come alive through the new technology in film making.

In the political world, the "Lewinsky Scandal" was happening in Washington. News that President Clinton was having an affair with Monica Lewinsky, a White House intern, first broke on January 17, 1998. Clinton stood in front of the American public and stated that he "did not have sexual relations with that woman."

Throughout the year, people debated on whether or not they thought the president really had an affair.

Evidence was turned over by Lewinsky and an investigation was held. It led to the impeachment of Clinton later that year by the U.S. House of Representatives and his subsequent acquittal on all charges of perjury and obstruction of justice in a twenty-one day Senate trial. Clinton admitted in August that he had an "improper physical relationship." In December he was acquitted of all charges and remained in office to carry out his second term.

From February 1996 to April 1999, there had been at least fourteen school shootings across the United States. Bomb threats and shootings caused the normally peaceful and safe environments of schools to be filled with fear and insecurity for students, teachers, and administrators. Mildred heard of local schools having bomb threats, including the high school that her granddaughter, Renee, attended. They had bomb threats almost once a day for over a week. It proved to Mildred that this society and these young people would grow up in a world very different from hers. On April 20, 1999, the Columbine High School massacre in Jefferson County, Colorado, was committed by two seniors who killed twelve students, one teacher, and injured twenty-one others before committing suicide. This raised debate over gun control, school safety, and bullying in schools across the nation.

Kids in the nineties were wearing baggy jeans, had tattoos and piercings, and were listening to rap, rock, and hip-hop. Popular toys hit the market as the economy boomed in the nineties. People were fighting over Beanie Babies, Furbies, and Tickle Me Elmo's in the stores, especially if their child had those items on their Christmas list.

The coming of the New Year of 2000 brought fear to all. With talk of system shut downs, and with the nation now being run by computers, people feared that systems would not know how to roll over from 1999 to the new millennium, 2000. Others talked it up by saying that the end of the world would come.

Mildred's family at her 80th birthday party at Steele Creek Park in Bristol

Trip to Richmond Confederate Museum with Renee to see Mildred's grandfather's Confederate flag in 1998

Trip to Myrtle Beach in 1994 with Linda, Patty, and Renee

One of first times wearing shorts

Christmas 1996 at Patty's

Mildred playing piano for Christmas 1997 in her home

Mildred in front of her childhood church, Green Spring

Family Reunion 1994
Mildred with "Her Fortune"

Family reunion 1995

Chapter 10

A New Century

Only a few minor glitches were caused by Y2K. Mildred celebrated New Year's with Linda's family. The power stayed on, computers continued to work, and just like every year since 1972, she along with the nation watched the ball drop in Time Square on Dick Clark's New Year's Rockin' Eve on TV.

> *"Went to Linda's at 7:30 p.m. Renee came from a party at 9 p.m. We ate finger food at 9:30. Talked and watched TV. Watched the old year out and the new year in at 12 o'clock. The Millennium 2000. All predictions failed."*
>
> —January 1, 2000

Mildred turned eighty-nine in 2000. She still lived alone and did her own house cleaning, cooking, and drove to the store and to get her hair fixed. She enjoyed friends and family, and talked on the phone regularly.

> *"Went to Ruth's at 9 a.m., then went to Food City for milk, etc. Went to Dollar Store. Got Whopper Jr. and brought home to eat."*
>
> —March 23, 2000

> *"Cooked these lovely beets. Peeled them then canned 10 pts. and have a lot more for tomorrow. They are so pretty. Red as can be."*
>
> —July 27, 2000

Mildred watched friends and family die in the following years. She became the last living classmate of her Stonewall Jackson

Alumni and the last cousin in her family. She saw those younger than her die, and sometimes wondered why she was here and others younger had to go. She knew God's plan however had given her a life of happiness, and she had no regrets. It really hit hard when she lost her grandson Greg, at the age of forty in 2001. She stood strong as she did all the other times of grief, and was strong for her son and his family.

In 2001, Mildred took her last trip to Salt Lake City to see Jimmy and Anne. She and Patty boarded a plane and flew there and back. They went just in time before the event of the century happened, which would detour people from wanting to travel by air.

The decade started with a War on Terror, when on September 11, 2001, Americans watched attacks on the home front. It was a day that would be remembered forever by all Americans, another day of events that people would recall as they had the death of President Kennedy.

Mildred was at home watching TV when she heard the news. A plane had flown into the World Trade Center in New York City. As she watched the news coverage, another plane flew into the second tower. In the mean time, a third plane hit the Pentagon and the fourth crashed in a field in Pennsylvania. Reports later confirmed that Al-Qaeda terrorists had hijacked all four planes. There were no survivors in all four crashes. Over 3,000 victims died in the attacks including firefighters, police officers, and first responders.

In the following months, memorial services were held and all over America, people hung their flags to show patriotism and honor for those who died. President George W. Bush announced to America that the U.S. was going to war. On October 7, U.S. and British forces initiated aerial bombing campaigns in Afghanistan, targeting Taliban and Al-Qaeda camps. Special forces later sent in ground troops and invaded Afghanistan. The hunt for Osama bin Laden, leader of Al-Qaeda, was underway.

September 18, 2001, started a scare for Americans when warnings were sent out that Anthrax was being spread through the mail system. Five people died who had received letters containing Anthrax spores. All were sent to news media offices in the U.S.

On September 30, 2001, Mildred celebrated her 90th birthday. She had a reception at the church for her friends and church family. The most memorable event that took place on her birthday occurred when she and her five children and granddaughter Renee spent the night in her childhood home in Green Spring.

The Lowry house had been purchased and renovated by a local couple who wanted to preserve the family memories that lay in the walls, and open a bed and breakfast. They invited Mildred and her family to spend the night, where Mildred got to sleep in the same room she slept in as a child. Memories filled her head that night. The next day, all the grandchildren and great-grandchildren came to spend the day and celebrate with a meal, cake, and gifts.

In 2002, the largest business scandal of the decade took place, when Enron and Worldcom collapsed in late 2001 and early 2002, exposing fraud and corruption in their management. The company's bosses were put on trial and their bankers were fired or fined. Thousands of investors lost a total of $240 billion.

Space exploration continued to evolve into the new century. Although news coverage was not as constant as it was back in the sixties when Americans were first hearing of man going into space, people were still fascinated with the new discoveries being found. N.A.S.A.'s first Mars exploration rover, known as Spirit, landed on Mars on January 4, 2004. The exploration was conducted to determine if life had ever existed on Mars.

On February 4, 2004, Facebook was founded. This social networking website was launched by a Harvard University student, and first became popular with colleges throughout the U.S. In years following, it became the largest social network in the world, and Internet lovers young and old started communicating via

Facebook.

It was the Internet that heavily influenced globalization throughout the world in the 2000's. It made it possible for people to interact with other people by expressing ideas and experiencing other cultures. Selling and buying online changed commerce forever, and online dating services forever changed the way couples communicated. The percent of marriages from online sites steadily increased in the 2000's. Chat rooms, Facebook, and My Space were popular social websites started in the decade. Ebay, Youtube, and Amazon were websites that many used to find that childhood toy, cheap book, or favorite song. Cell phones were now purchased with the Internet, text messaging, music, and movies at your fingertips.

In 2004, a tsunami was generated from an earthquake that hit Southeast Asia, killing 200,000 and displacing millions. Not long after that devastation, another environmental disaster hit, this time in the U.S. Hurricane Katrina first hit the Bahamas, before crossing into Florida and into Louisiana. The levee system in New Orleans, meant to protect from floods, broke in the violent storm and flooded the city. After the hurricane had passed, 1,836 were killed either from the storm or the flood. Around eighty percent of residents were still in New Orleans when the levee broke, aiming much criticism toward the Bush administration and the U.S. Federal Emergency Management Agency.

Medical history was made in the 2000's when the first face transplant occurred in France, the first premature baby had open-heart surgery, and a blind person was fitted with electronic eyes.

Happy times and sad times filled the years. Carter Jr. got divorced and later remarried in 2007 to Kate Macdonald who gave Mildred two step-grandchildren and two step-great-grandchildren. Mildred rejoiced in the good times as she now watched great-grandchildren and her last grandchild get married. Patty retired from Burlington Industries in 2004, and Linda had been working for the Department of Human Services in Bristol since 1999.

In 2007, Mildred decided to give up her driver's license. Her little Celebrity would sit in her basement garage, where she went down to start it up every once in a while and shine it.

> *"My 96th Birthday. What a surprise. Pat and I went to church then here came my family... We ate at Fishtales and was so nice. One big long table. They served so nicely. Beautiful cake, etc. A wonderful surprise Birthday."*
>
> —Sunday, Sept. 30, 2007.

> *"Linda took off early and took me to get a flu shot and she got hers. Then to Wal-Mart to get medicine and groceries. I rode the little electric cart around. It's fun."*
>
> —Oct. 26, 2007

As the end of the decade neared, in 2007, the credit crunch began. Many large financial institutes collapsed when they were unable to call in massive debts. Stock markets fell across the world. Assets began to drop dramatically in value. This all led to an economic crisis in the U.S. The industrial world entered an economic recession. People lost their houses, stores closed, and millions lost their jobs.

The economic crisis was given hope when the first African American ran for office and used the slogan "Change we can believe in." Barack Obama, senator from Illinois, pushed for American withdrawal from Iraq, universal health care as top national priority, increasing energy independence, and getting the nation out of the economic crisis. He defeated Republican John McCain, and became the 44th President of the United States in 2009.

In 2010, Mildred was still going strong. Even though she had hardships and times where she did not feel well, she kept going. She continued to travel and live in her house, cleaning and cooking.

She showed great strength in her older age. In September

2009, her youngest grandson Stephen died at the age of forty-one. It was sudden. Even though she was in shock, just as when her husband died, she was strong and was supportive to her son Jimmy and his wife Anne.

Continuing her travels in 2010, Mildred took a trip with Carter Jr., Kate, and Patty to Branson, Missouri. They took the deep southern route back home so they could stop in and see Renee and her husband Jason in Meridian, Mississippi, where they had just moved.

Not long after that trip, in September 2010, Carter Jr. had a massive heart attack and was put in ICU. Not knowing whether he was going to make it or not, Linda went up to tell Mildred. The first thing Mildred did was go to her closet and find something nice to wear to see Carter. She wanted to see him. She went to the hospital almost every day that week. He recovered and was discharged the day before attending Mildred's birthday party.

Mildred celebrated her 99th birthday on September 30, 2010. Her children planned a big event at Windsor Avenue Presbyterian Church, where over one hundred friends and family gathered to wish her a Happy Birthday.

Mildred's 90th birthday at her home place, The Lowry House

Mildred on the front porch with Carter Jr., Linda, Patty, and Gene

Mildred going to bed in her childhood bedroom

Next to her childhood playhouse

Mildred with Oma Hall

Five generations in 2004:
Mildred, son Gene, granddaughter Angela, great-grandson Adam, and great-great-granddaughter Aiyana

Bringing in the New Year 2007 with grape juice

2008 family reunion at Carter Jr.'s

Mildred on her 99th birthday

Chapter 11

A Century Old

On January 1, 2011, Mildred called her granddaughter Renee to wish her a Happy New Year. During that phone conversation, she stated that she stayed up to midnight to watch the ball drop. The last thing she remembered was the crowd counting down to nine, then she fell asleep. When she woke up, the new year was here. She had been born in 1911 and now had seen the year 2011 arrive.

Over the one hundred years that she has lived, she has seen eighteen presidents in office, many natural disasters, and man walk on the moon. She has seen the telephone go from a box on the wall to a hand held device, and communication go from writing a letter to sending an electronic message across country in a second.

She had seen African Americans be forced to sit in the back of a bus, to an African American sitting in the seat of President of the United States.

Not only had the nation changed, but so had her family. She had seen her parents, husband, and all her cousins pass away, along with two grandsons. She knew what it was to have hard times. She had financial hardships, troubled relationships, and health issues in her life.

The *Titanic* that sunk in 1912, was the subject of a major motion picture in 1997. War had been happening for one hundred years across the world. She had heard her grandfather talk about brother against brother in the Civil War, and later in her own life, knew what it was like for her country to be in turmoil.

She had seen the depression of the thirties, and a recession in the 2000's. She saw her father drive a Model T Ford in the Twenties, and later her son drive a home on wheels in the eighties.

In 2011 she watched the son of Princess Diana, Prince

William, marry Kate Middleton. They drove down the same street where fourteen years earlier, William had walked behind his mother's coffin.

Disaster after disaster had happened all over the world in one hundred years, and in 2011, she saw the worst outbreak of tornadoes occur in history. The "Super Outbreak" occurred from April 25 to 28, as a total of 334 tornadoes broke out across twenty-one states from Texas to New York. Tennessee was one state that was hit. Mildred stayed up all night watching the weather and getting her purse and flashlight ready to go to the basement. It thankfully did not affect her or her family, but over three hundred people were killed as a result of the storms.

Mildred saw much change in one hundred years. It can be argued as to whether it was good change or bad. Life will never be as calm and simple as it had been in her childhood.

She calls her children her fortune as they provide for her and take care of her. She often reminisces about the past. She says that she lives on memories. When asked what contributed to her living such a long life, she will answer by saying, "I was always happy. I had a happy childhood, a happy marriage, and happy old age."

THE WHITE HOUSE
WASHINGTON

Happy 100th Birthday! We wish you the very best on this momentous occasion.

You have witnessed great milestones in our Nation's history, and your life represents an important part of the American story. As you reflect upon a century of memories, we hope that you are filled with tremendous pride and joy.

Congratulations on your birthday, and may you enjoy many more happy years as a centenarian.

Sincerely,

Barack Obama Michelle Obama

Bibliography

Britten, Loretta, and Sarah Brash. *The American Dream: The 50's.* Richmond, VA: Time Life Inc., 1998.

Brokaw, Tom. *Boom! : Talking about the sixties.* New York: Random House, 2007.

Confederate Veteran 25. 5. (1917).

Davis, Kenneth C. *Don't Know Much About History.* New York: Crown Publishers Inc., 1990.

Dershowitz, Alan M. *America on Trial: Inside the legal battles that transformed our nation.* Warner Books, 2004.

Harvey Jr. and Edmund H. *Our Glorious Century.* New York: The Reader's Digest Association, Inc., 1994.

Igloo. *History Through Headlines.* Igloo Books Ltd., 2009.

Stone, George and Sonya A. Haskins. *Images of America: Bristol.* Charleston, SC: Arcadia Publishing, 2005.

The Farm Journal 40. 8. (1916): 29.

The Ganzel Group Communications. "Farming in the 1940's." Wessels Living History Farm. Feb. 2011 http://www.livinghistoryfarm.org

Truman, Harry S. *The Autobiography of Harry S. Truman.* Boulder, CO: Colorado Associated University Press, 1980.

Warmuth, Donna Akers. *Images of America: Abingdon Virginia.* Charleston, SC: Arcadia Publishing, 2002.

About the Author

Renee Reed Gilliam was born and raised in Bristol, Tennessee. She is a 2006 graduate of Milligan College, where she received her Bachelor of Science degree in Communications with an emphasis in Journalism and a minor in History. She earned her Master of Education degree in 2009.

Renee and her husband Jason live in Mooresville, NC where she owns and operates Little Hoot Publishing, LLC. This is the first book Renee has written and published.

CPSIA information can be obtained at www.ICGtesting.com
Printed in the USA
BVOW030458250113

311572BV00001B/2/P